KW-064-678

CARING FOR CHILDREN
IN TROUBLE

INTERNATIONAL LIBRARY OF SOCIOLOGY AND SOCIAL RECONSTRUCTION

Founded by Karl Mannheim
Editor W. J. H. Sprott

A catalogue of books available in the INTERNATIONAL LIBRARY OF SOCIOLOGY AND SOCIAL RECONSTRUCTION and new books in preparation for the Library will be found at the end of this volume

Caring for Children in Trouble

JULIUS CARLEBACH

LONDON

ROUTLEDGE & KEGAN PAUL

NEW YORK: HUMANITIES PRESS

Published in Great Britain 1970
by Routledge and Kegan Paul Ltd
Broadway House, 68–74 Carter Lane
London, E.C.4
Printed in Great Britain by
The Camelot Press Ltd
London and Southampton
© Julius Carlebach 1970
No part of this book may be reproduced
in any form without permission from
the publisher, except for the quotation
of brief passages in criticism
SBN 7100 6564 7

Contents

CONTENTS

vi

Acknowledgements

This book is the result of a long-standing interest in the development of institutional child care and of a specific research project carried out in the University of Cambridge from 1964–1966. It gives me great pleasure to acknowledge the debt of gratitude I owe to the many people and organizations who have assisted me. To Professor W. A. Lloyd and Mr. F. H. McClintock for their help and encouragement. To the managers of approved schools who have co-operated in the survey, many of whom have gone out of their way to supply information. To members of the Home Office Research Unit and Children's Department who have also supplied valuable information.

My special thanks are also due to the managers of the Philanthropic Society School; Lt. Col. H. Glanfield the former Director of the Children's Aid Society; Mr. H. Cohen of Finnart House School; the Curator of the Red Lodge Museum in Bristol; Dr. T. Morris and the Librarian of the London School of Economics; the Public Record Office and the Librarians of the Universities of London and Cambridge, who have all been most helpful in securing rare and obscure materials for this study.

I have received very helpful advice and criticisms of various sections of this study from Mr. John Gittins; Mr. Richard Balbernie; Professor Michael Banton; Mr. G. F. Pettit; Mr. Alan Jacka; but most of all from Dr. Peter Scott. I am also indebted to Mrs. B. Browse for secretarial assistance.

For financial help during the full-time research I am greatly indebted to Mrs. J. C. Burkill; The Lady Rachel Lauterpacht; the Trustees of the Haendler Trust and the Master and Fellows of Emmanuel College, Cambridge.

To Myrna

Introduction

Residential institutions have been studied in a number of different ways. A popular early method was to study the inmates of institutions and to define institutional function and organization as products of the sum of the problems presented by the inmates.[1] More recently different and more meaningful approaches have been used. American prison studies, culminating in Goffman's essay on total institutions,[2] have suggested a corporate life for institutions which is independent of individual inmates or members of staff, and have clarified the internal structure of institutions by analysing staff and inmates as interacting groups. Another approach has been derived from operational research in which institutions are subjected to analysis of their internal structure and function with the object of evaluating these in terms of efficiency and effectiveness. Such an approach has been used to great advantage by authors like Sofer.[3] Yet another method has been developed for institutions having highly specialized ideologies in which the whole unit is seen in relation to its objective of achieving an effect on inmates and which directly intervenes in the normal staff/inmate structure, as for example in studies of therapeutic communities.[4] Theoretical models for institutions also exist. An example is Howard Jones's model of the approved school system in which he endeavours to explain the friction between staff and inmates by using Vold's conflict theory.[5] Such an explanation might

[1] The classic examples of this approach are the books of Mary Carpenter (see below) which confirm the principle suggested by Kirkman Gray that institutional function precedes institutional organization. See B. Kirkman Gray, *A History of English Philanthropy*, London, 1905, p. 158.

[2] Cf. D. Clemmer, *The Prison Community*, 1940, G. S. Sykes, *The Society of Captives*, London, 1958, and E. Goffman, *On the Characteristics of Total Institutions in Asylum*, New York, 1961.

[3] C. Sofer, *The Organization from Within*, London, 1961.

[4] See R. Rapoport, *The Community as Doctor*, London, 1960.

[5] H. Jones, 'The Approved School – A Theoretical Model in Sociological Studies in the British Penal Services', *Soc. Rev. Monogr.* ix. Ed. Paul Halmos, 1965, pp. 99–110.

have been more convincing if Bradley had not described a 'natural enmity' theory between public school boys and teachers one hundred years previously.[1]

In this study an attempt has been made to utilize another dimension for the study of institutions[2] and the origin of this approach can be briefly outlined as follows. For the past twenty-five years there has been a steady decline in the success rates for boys in approved schools. The usual explanation offered for this phenomenon is that because the Courts have a much wider range of treatment facilities for boys appearing before them, only the 'worst' find their way into approved schools and one would therefore expect the more sensitive classification used by the Courts to be mirrored in the schools' rates of success. It will be shown that this explanation is inadequate and has in fact been used continuously throughout this century though not exclusively to explain falling success rates. I have argued therefore that if the characteristics of the boys do not explain a falling success rate, a partial explanation may be found in the way the approved school system is operated. Inasmuch as the system is now 113 years old it seemed essential to understand how the system has developed and the forces which have led to changes and alterations. In order to study this I have gone back to the first institution in this country which concerned itself with the rehabilitation of young offenders and have traced the history of institutions to ascertain how far they have determined their own function, how far such functions were determined by social pressures in the environments in which the institutions operated and how far the explicit and theoretical formulations of men and women involved in institutional work were able to determine their functions and their organization. It appears that the basic internal problems of institution were made explicit after relatively short experience but, because institutions are subject to pressures from persons and events over which they have no control, they are unable to develop policies by resolving difficulties systematically and in the light of experience. Instead they are frequently moved into

[1] A. G. Bradley, *A History of Marlborough College*, London, 1893, p. 72. Bradley claimed that this theory was fashionable in 1843.

[2] The method has already been used effectively by Roger Hood. See *Borstal Re-assessed*, London, 1965.

extreme positions, or influenced by irrelevant factors which stem from climates of opinion outside the institution.

My aim in the present study has been to show by detailed historical analysis how the present approved school system has evolved and how it has been subjected to forces of change which have denied the schools a real chance of remaining fully effective. In a final section I have permitted myself the luxury of expressing some very personal views on the problems of change in the residential care of children and young people based not only on the main text but also on my own experience as a practitioner and teacher in the field.

Chapter 1

Prototypes: Pioneers and Principles

I THE PHILANTHROPIC SOCIETY

Historical studies of institutions dealing with delinquent children are very inadequate when one compares them, for example, with histories of public schools. Institutions for children have existed for several centuries;[1] and although the Marine Society is generally regarded as the first attempt to deal with semi-delinquent youth, it was never an institution *per se*.[2] The Magdalen Hospital, which was established by Jonas Hanway in 1758, could also be regarded as an institution for what might today be called delinquent girls, but since it was established exclusively for sexually wayward girls, it does not really fall into the field of this investigation.[3] The institution quite properly regarded as the first to be established in this country for delinquent and semi-delinquent children was the Philanthropic Society.

As one of the two prototypal institutions for delinquents in this country its early history deserves to be better known, yet even the Society itself does not appear to have made a comprehensive study of its own origins. This is in marked contrast, for example, to the first French and German institutions, the Agricultural Colony at Mettray and the Rauhe Haus near Hamburg.[4]

[1] Mary Hopkirk, *Nobody Wanted Sam*. London, 1949. Story of the unwelcomed child, 1530–1948.
[2] C. E. B. Russell, *The Making of the Criminal*, London, 1906, pp. 202–203.
[3] B. Kirkman Gray, op. cit., pp. 164–5.
[4] Thus, the library of the University of Hamburg has eleven major publications on Wichern and the Rauhe Haus, which were published since

4

The early years

On 5 September 1788, Robert Young called a meeting at his house to discuss the plight of the vagrant and destitute children who abounded in London.[1] The kind of children this meeting was concerned with can best be illustrated by examples from the admission register of the Society.[2]

Boy 12	No father, mother partly begs and sells matches. Boy found naked and starved.
Boy (age unknown)	Orphaned, found begging – almost starved.
Boy 12	No father or mother – found begging – almost naked.
Boy 7	Orphan found almost starved, not knowing where he belongs.
Boy 8	Mother beat him – left him for dead – found by workman and adopted. Then taught to steal by thieves.
Girl 9	Father transported, mother used to 'let' girl to woman for begging.
Girl 12	Mother common prostitute, now dead. Girl in state of poverty and wretchedness.
Girl 14	Mother transported. Girl taken from a house of ill fame.
Girl 9	Mother dead, father transported for robbery.

To offer help to such children, the meeting decided to form a society which was to be called the *New Asylum for the Prevention of Vice and Misery among the Poor*. Young was appointed

---

1927. There is no single publication on the Philanthropic Society or Redhill School apart from a small centenary booklet *The Philanthropic Society: Centenary Report 1888* and another small pamphlet *The Royal Philanthropic Society 1788–1953* published on the 150th anniversary. Neither of these appear to have made real use of the Society's extensive archives which go back to 1788 and which are now in the care of the Surrey County Archivist.

[1] This and all subsequent details of the Society are taken from the Abstracts of the Proceedings of the Philanthropic Society from 1788 onwards. These are handwritten volumes. The writer examined them while they were stored in an attic in the Warden's House at Redhill.

[2] 'Character of Boys admitted to the Reform 1788'. 'Character of Girls admitted to the Reform 1788'.

Intendant and the Marquis of Carmarthen elected President.[1] The meeting also resolved that if any building were to be put up for the care of such children there should be no surrounding walls in order to make a clear distinction between an 'asylum' and a 'prison'. Money was to be collected from the public.

The first children taken into the care of the Society were sent out to foster parents but when the number of children had reached twelve the Society rented a small house for £10 a year, put a matron in charge and placed the children there to be taught to knit stockings and to make lace. Further houses were quickly taken over and tradesmen and their wives were made responsible for the care of the children. Thus one house had a shoemaker, another a tailor and a third a carpenter.[2]

Within two years, however, it became clear that Mr. Young was perhaps not all that he appeared to be. The committee called on him to produce his accounts, whereupon he resigned his treasurership. It was probably in 1790 that the name 'Philanthropic Society' was adopted and the Duke of Leeds elected President.[3] When Young eventually appeared before the committee he was reported to be owing the Society the sum of £1,811 1s. 7¼d. Young was dismissed from all offices in the Society and the committee appointed four 'visitors' to supervise the children's homes.[4] Through the good offices of the City of London, the Society acquired some property at St. George's Fields, Southwark, in 1792 and an institution was opened there;[5] dormitories and workshops were set up with provisions for teaching tailoring, shoemaking, printing, bookbinding and ropemaking. A separate section was set aside for girls who were to be taught needlework and work in the laundry and kitchen. Admission was restricted to two classes of children. Those who were 'offspring of felons' which usually meant that, with one or

---

[1] Abstract 01 (September 1788).

[2] These first cottages were situated in Hackney.

[3] The choice of name may possibly have been influenced by the rapid spread on the Continent of Europe of Basedow's 'Philanthropinum' – a type of school not unlike what the Philanthropic had in mind. J. R. H. Quick, *Essays on Educational Reformers*, London, 1898, pp. 278–85.

[4] Abstract 01.

[5] 'Memorial of Certain Persons calling themselves the Philanthropic Society to the Rt. Hon. William Pitt', December 1795.

both parents executed, transported or imprisoned, the children were destitute, in addition to being presumed 'tainted' by their contact with criminal parents. The second category was of those children who had themselves been involved in crime. To begin with, convicted children were not separated from children who had not undergone the processes of the law. The Reverend Dr. Gregory was appointed as the first chaplain superintendent. The new institution also had a section which was set aside as a 'prison' (this meant the introduction of cells which are later referred to as a means of punishment), and a special building for newly admitted boys who passed through a probationary period before being moved into the general institution.[1] Within four years, therefore, the Society had established a full-scale institution for delinquent and semi-delinquent children of both sexes. As yet very little attention had been given to the question of staffing, but by congregating large numbers of children in one institution problems of discipline and control became inevitable. The committee ordered conduct books to be kept and evening schools to be established for the children. The first chaplain superintendent lasted less than a year, and his successor, the Reverend Durant, was dismissed soon after his appointment because, during his short reign, the girls as well as the boys were guilty of serious misconduct. To add to the Society's troubles, Mr. Young, the disgraced founder, was still sending out collectors for a society with a very similar name, and the committee was forced to publish warnings about Young's activities in the Press.[2]

The lack of experience of the managers of the institution led them to spend rather more on food and clothing for the children than they could properly afford. As a result, in 1793 a special committee was set up to investigate expenditure. Food was cut by buying milk diluted in a proportion of two quarts of water to one pint of milk, the cheese supper allowance was cut and the free access to 'small beer' for the boys was stopped.[3] At the same

[1] Almost every institution in the nineteenth century made use of such 'probationary periods'. Their significance will be discussed later. Abstract o2 (18 April 1793).

[2] Advertisements were placed in the *Morning Chronicle*, *The Times*, *True Briton*, *Public Advertiser*, *Gazetteer*, *Morning Herald*, *Oracle*, *Star*, *Sun*, *Observer*. Abstract o2 (26 April 1793).

[3] Abstract o2 (3 May 1793).

time the green uniforms were changed to plain coarse canvas and the trimming of the girls' hats was done away with.[1] At the annual dinner for the Society,

> . . . the children in the Society's protection walked in procession around the room, first upwards of 30 girls presented by their mistress. After this, near on 100 boys, each department led by respective masters, the carpenter, printer, shoemaker and tailor. The decent appearance and orderly demeanour of the children filled the minds of the spectators with the most pleasant sensation; the natural result of contemplating the happy change which had been wrought in the institution of this numerous little group lately in the high road of vice.[2]

The pattern of the houses in the institution had now been established, each house having a master and mistress and forty-five boys, with a basement equipped with kitchen, pantry, washhouse and cells. The boys acted as apprentices to the masters; those who absconded were taken before a magistrate as 'refractory apprentices'.[3]

By 1794 it was found that a system of rewarding well-behaved boys was effective. Corporal punishment is not mentioned in the early records of the Society, but cells were used frequently 'with bread and water' although this punishment could only be imposed by one of the 'visitors'.[4] In that year it was decided to engage a matron who was to 'superintend and direct the conduct of the cook, take care of the boys' linen, mend their

---

[1] Even so, the Society's standards were very good compared with the early years of some public schools. 'Accommodation was often primitive and the food not only unappetising but . . . insufficient. Quite unmanageable numbers were herded into a single school room. . . . At night the dormitories were so crowded that two or three slept in one bed. . . .' See J. Ogilvie, *The English Public School*, London, 1957, p. 124.

[2] Abstract 02 (18 April 1793).

[3] Abstract 02 (7 June 1793). The detention of children without legal sanction was one of the most difficult problems institutions had to deal with. This method, developed by the Philanthropic, was later adopted by the magistrates for Stretton on Dunsmore. Another system, used by the Magdalen Hospital, was to make the girl pay £10 maintenance if she left within three years. But it is difficult to see how this could have worked with destitute girls. B. Kirkman Gray, op. cit., p. 165.

[4] Abstract 03 (April 1794).

8

stockings, act as nurse whenever any of the children are ill, take the young boys under her particular care, and see that the children and their dormitories are kept perfectly clean and neat'.[1]

The girls lived in the section of the institution at Bermondsey, whilst the boys were at St. George's Fields. The boys wore a tin badge marked 'Philanthropic Society' on each arm and received half a pint of beer each at dinner and at supper. They appear to have been fairly rough as we may gather from the following Committee order dated 13 June 1794:

> Ordered that the boys be not permitted to go into the country for a holiday unless the superintendent and masters see that they have no weapons as guns, pistols, etc., of any sort; and that they behave themselves with the greatest regularity and never enter into any gardens, orchards, pleasure grounds, etc., by which they could give offence or do any mischief and that they be always present with some of the masters. . . .

otherwise this 'indulgence' was to be stopped.[2] In that year it was also decided to stop the bonfire on 5 November.

The girls were sent out at a very young age as 'menial servants' although the Society was most careful to see that the mistresses of the girls were of the best character.[3]

The Society attempted in 1794 to obtain government support because in May of that year there was an application before Parliament 'for the purpose of constructing a penitentiary house for the reception and employment of such adult criminals whose crimes are not of sufficient malignity to subject them to transportation'. As the Society were 'providing for the reformation and instruction of criminal infants', they felt that their work would fall within the new scheme.[4]

This request does not appear to have been successful and in December 1795 a memorial was presented to William Pitt,

---

[1] Abstract 03 (Sub-Committee Rep. 9 May 1794).

[2] If our assumption is right that the Philanthropic tried to model itself in some ways on Basedow's Philanthropinum, such walks would be very much in character. Abstract 03 (June 1794).

[3] Thus, they refused an application from a woman seeking a servant on the grounds that the woman kept a lodging house. Abstract 03 (19 December 1794).

[4] Abstract 03 (16 May 1794).

Bc

calling on the government to assist the Society in relieving its financial distress.[1]

The petition is of interest because it now clearly described the function of the Society as seen by its managers. The Society existed

. . . for the purpose of receiving the destitute infant children of convicts, and to rescue them from vice and infamy to which the example and sentence of their parents exposed them and for the reform of such young criminals whose youth gave promise of amendment by impressing upon their minds principles of morality and religion and instructing them in useful occupations to enable them to gain an honest livelihood and become beneficial members of society.

In the absence of Parliamentary support, the Society's finances were seriously strained. No children were admitted in 1795; their clothes were further reduced in colour and quality, and working hours were increased to be equal to those worked by ordinary apprentices in the country. The children were divided into classes although it is not at all clear on what basis the classification was made. It is possible that since it was first mentioned in relation to bread rationing that it was a classification by age. Thus the boys had three classes, receiving $2\frac{1}{2}$, 2, and $1\frac{1}{2}$ quartern loaves of bread per week respectively, whilst the girls were divided into two classes receiving 2 and $1\frac{1}{2}$ quartern loaves per week.[2]

In 1796 a special Sub-Committee of the Philanthropic Society was appointed to examine the state of the Society and to report on its first seven years and the 176 boys and 60 girls[3] who had been admitted to it.

[1] 'The Memorial of Certain Persons calling themselves the Philanthropic Society'. In it the Society argued that between 1788 and 1794 they had admitted 288 children who would otherwise have become 'prostitutes or thieves'. The cost had been £23,000. Of this, £19,000 had been subscribed by voluntary donations and £2,500 had been profit on the children's work. In addition, they had spent £9,000 on buildings but received only £5,000 in contributions. There was a debt therefore of some £5,500 and it is this amount which they asked from Parliament (23 December 1795).

[2] Abstract 04 (December 1795).

[3] In their petition the Society claimed to have dealt with 288 children though the Sub-Committee report shows that this was only 236 children.

Dealing with the boys first, the Committee[1] reported that of 176 boys, 51 had absconded. This figure illustrates the difficulty experienced by the voluntary institutions in holding on to their charges without legal powers. Seventeen had gone to sea, 5 had been sent to the Marine Society, 3 were expelled, 10 had returned to their families, 7 were placed in employment and 3 had died; 80 boys were still in the institution. It was noted that of the 51 absconders, 31 had been aged thirteen or more at the time they were admitted and the Committee suggested that boys of thirteen and over should not in future be admitted, because at that age they were 'so far advanced in years as affording little chance of their being reclaimed'. The Committee further suggested that boys 'who manifest vicious dispositions' should be kept separate from other boys and where possible removed from the institution. No boy should be dismissed without fair trial, but once it had become clear that he would not mend his ways, the interests of the other boys, no less than those who supported the institution financially, demanded that such youngsters be removed.

This was not to say, of course, that those boys who had remained and who were regarded as being capable of reform would always behave in an exemplary fashion. The Committee recommended that regular reports about the behaviour of the boys should be made by the masters, and submitted to the Committee by the superintendent. It was felt that in this way the concern of the staff might be enhanced. The Committee also recommended that small rewards should be available for boys who behaved well.

It was intended to extend this behaviour control system to the girls also. Of the 60 girls who had been admitted, 5 had absconded, 7 had been placed in employment, one had died and 40 were still in the institution. The behaviour of the girls was rather better than that of the boys, because 'many of them were received in a state of childhood and innocence, the descendants of offending parents', though some of the girls had been convicted of pilfering and had been sent to the Society by magistrates. However, 'no one of this sex can be admitted or retained under any appearance of unchaste manners'. It was

---

[1] Report of the Committee Appointed to Examine the State of the Philanthropic Society, 1796. Abstract 04 (8 April 1796).

apparently very difficult to find suitable places for girls. Some of the difficulty appears to have been due to the heavy demands made on even the youngest girls, which were often sufficient to make the girls return to the Reform, although the Committee pointed out that a girl would not return to 'a life which the girls lead in their gloomy apartments in the Reform' if they had an even moderately comfortable position.

A striking illustration of this problem is contained in the Society's Register of Admissions.[1] Mary Smith was admitted to the Reform on 14 December 1792 at the age of nine years – described as an

artful and depraved character. The person under whose protection she had been, having often found it necessary to correct her, died, and during the time he was in his coffin, she stole an opportunity, unseen, of getting into the room, uncovered the sheet and spoke to the corpse in these terms – 'I don't mind you – you can't hurt me now'.

The girls were employed in 'making and mending their own gowns, doing their own linen and that of the boys, washing of same, the stockings, sheets and house linen and keeping the house clean', whilst the boys were employed as follows:

34 with the shoemaker,
20 in the rope walk,
10 with the tailor,
6 in the printing office,
3 with the cook,
2 at the gates,
1 with the steward,
4 too young for any employment.

The diet of the children was:

Breakfast: bread, milk and water
Dinner
    Monday: broth and potatoes (no bread)
    Tuesday: the meat of which Monday's broth was made and potatoes
    Wednesday: puddings of potatoes and flour
    Thursday: legs of beef stewed and potatoes

[1] Admission Register 1789–1806.

Friday: beef and mutton and potatoes stewed
Saturday: rice pudding
Sunday: boiled beef and potatoes
Lunch: bread with milk and water
bread and cheese.

The girls had the same as the boys except that they had rice and milk on Tuesday instead of meat, but this appears to have disagreed with them and they were given rice pudding instead.

All the children were taught to read the New Testament every evening.

This report highlights what were destined to become and to remain some of the dominant factors determining the success or failure of an institution, namely, the nature of the admissions, classification of inmates within the institution, the problem of discipline, the involvement of staff within the institution and disposal after training.

In 1797 the Committee introduced an experiment which was many years later to become one of the outstanding characteristics of the French institution at Mettray. A meeting on 17 March of that year resolved that

the secretary send the names of the children who had been apprenticed out to such members of the Society as resided in the neighbourhood where the particular apprentices are in service, and that the said members be requested to accept the office of guardian of the said children; and that they call on them from time to time and admonish them when necessary; and report on their conduct at every quarterly meeting.[1]

This probably represents the first recorded attempt to introduce aftercare.

In that year the Committee also decided not to admit children under the age of eight except in very urgent cases.[2]

Towards the end of the century both boys and girls continued to be troublesome. Elaborate plans were made to prevent boys from absconding; the visits of parents were strictly controlled and it was decided that porters should sleep in the boys' dormitories. The Committee also reported riots by the girls. In 1799 the Duke of York took over the Presidency of the Society.[3] At

---

[1] Abstract 05.   [2] Ibid.   [3] Abstract 06.

the turn of the nineteenth century, the house at Bermondsey was set aside as a Reform.[1]

In spite of various difficulties, the Society was now well established and in 1806 Parliament passed an 'Act for Establishing and Well Governing the Charitable Institution commonly called The Philanthropic Society'.[2]

The Society now adopted a change in dress for the boys according to seniority and apprenticeship and the matron was ordered to visit the girls in service half-yearly and to report on their well-being. There is a report (about 1810) on the removal of the Reform from Bermondsey to St. George's Fields, and at about the same time the Society refused an application by the Magistrate of Birmingham to establish a school 'for infant criminals'. After the Napoleonic Wars the boys appear to have been particularly difficult, and their 'turn-outs' (leave to go out) were suspended because of riots in London.[3]

In the period 1816–1820 the Society seems to have been troubled particularly by the girls, who were absconding and making attempts to communicate with the boys. After 13 girls absconded the sub-matron was dismissed, the matron admonished, and it was decided not to admit girls with criminal records in future.[4] Another 17 girls escaped shortly afterwards and a sub-committee appointed to investigate the incident reported that the escapes were due to 'the undue restraint of the girls'. It was decided, therefore, to ease the discipline. Girls were to be allowed to go out with the matron and occasionally to visit their relatives.[5] The matron resigned shortly afterwards because of 'ill health'.[6]

[1] Abstract 07.
[2] The full title of the Act reads: 'An Act for establishing and well-governing the charitable institution commonly called the Philanthropic Society formed for the Protection of Poor Children The Offspring of Convicted Felons, and for the Reformation of Children who have themselves been engaged in criminal practices.' A copy of the Act was published by the Philanthropic Society (St. George's Fields) in 1820.
[3] Abstract 08.   [4] Abstract 09 1817.   [5] Abstract 08.
[6] Excessive discipline for adolescent girls and the resultant explosions are a constant occurrence in nineteenth-century institutions. Yet not only did they not learn from the experiences of the Philanthropic, the practice was and perhaps still is common, although the basic principle had been expounded at least as long ago as 1580 by Montaigne: '. . . it is most true that one who has come safe with bag and baggage out of a free schooling inspires much more

The next twenty years were a period of steady, if not altogether successful, work. In 1824 a lending library was established for the children.[1] In 1826 a schoolmaster was appointed and the Committee made a recommendation to clergymen preaching in the chapel at St. George's Fields 'not to allude in sermons to the former states of the boys'. The boys continued to be troublesome.[2] They rioted occasionally and on one occasion even attacked the beadle, for which they forfeited their blue and brown clothes and the Society introduced solitary cells for work.[3]

A greater separation of younger and older boys was also ordered and boys were now punished for staying out at night.[4] Towards the end of the 1830s the Committee began to discuss the desirability of discontinuing the girls' section altogether. They also decided to do away with the monthly reward called 'good money'. In 1840 another special committee stated that the boys were not benefiting morally or generally from their training and further efforts were made to tighten the discipline of the school. A special sub-committee was also appointed to investigate and, if necessary, recommended the expulsion of, particularly 'bad boys'.[5]

The Duke of Richmond became the President of the Society in 1840 and in 1841 the Committee elected the Reverend Sydney Turner as the resident chaplain. With that appointment the influence of the Committee waned considerably. Turner put the Society on a sound footing and ensured its survival to the present day.

The Philanthropic under Sydney Turner

Sydney Turner[6] was one of the most important figures in the

---

confidence than one who comes safely out of a school in which she has been kept a strict prisoner' (*The Essays of Montaigne*, translated by E. J. Trechman, Oxford University Press, no date, Vol. li, p. 344).

[1] Abstract 11.   [2] Abstract 13.   [3] Abstracts 14 and 15.
[4] Abstract 15.   [5] Abstract 17.

[6] Turner was born in 1814. He was educated at Trinity College, Cambridge (1832–1836) where he took his B.A. degree in 1836 and his M.A. in 1839. In 1838 Turner was ordained by the Bishop of Winchester and was appointed curate at Christ Church, Southwark. In 1841 he was appointed Resident Chaplain and Reader of the Philanthropic Society School. Turner

English Reformatory Schools Movement. Like Jebb he has been largely ignored by British penologists in spite of his very considerable contribution to the education of delinquent juveniles. As resident chaplain at the Philanthropic Society School he produced a series of valuable reports on that institution, some of which will now be considered.

Turner's first report to the Committee of the Philanthropic Society was written six months after he had assumed office.[1] This report is concerned mainly with that part of the institution called 'The Manufactury' which dealt with those children who had not themselves been convicted of any criminal offence. He approached his task by making a careful analysis of the methods and techniques employed in the institution, but made it a principle not to introduce any sudden changes unless these were essential. He preferred to 're-model silently and gradually'. His review is presented under three headings: education, discipline, and employment.

Education

For an average of sixty boys aged from 11 to 16 the subjects taught were arithmetic, writing, spelling and reading (New Testament and SPCK publications). He thought that arithmetic and writing were well taught but found the reading deficient in content. Religious instruction 'exercised the memory rather than the mind'. He recommended that a wider range of books be used, an improved system of teaching and examination, and the use of visual aids. He subdivided the schoolroom with curtains and reorganized the classes. He also expressed a wish to extend education to the older boys. He proposed two objects in the education of the children; firstly, to make learning a thing of understanding and, secondly, to excite and exercise a taste for reading. To this end he increased the number and type

---

was appointed Inspector of Reformatory Schools in 1857, and in 1861 Industrial Schools also came under his inspection. He continued as senior inspector until 1875 when, for reasons of health, he resigned and accepted a nomination as Dean of Ripon. He remained there only one year and retired to the rectory of Hampsted in Gloucestershire where he died on 26 June 1879 at the age of 65 (*Annual Register*, New Series 1879, London 1880. *The Times*, 3 July 1879).

[1] Report December 1841.

of books in the library arguing that 'a taste for reading and a desire of acquiring information is seldom found combined with very low and degrading habits'.

The delinquents averaged twenty in number and most of these were below 13. He found the general standards to be lower, but relatively these boys were making better progress due to a good master, smaller numbers, and the lower age range of the group.

Turner described the education of the girls as very defective in matter and manner. House and laundry work should be regarded as part of the girls' education, but girls would be better prepared for domestic service and marriage if they were also taught to write and the basic principles of arithmetic. He suggested wide over-all improvements for the girls but, because of the lack of competent teachers for girls, he selected three of his best senior girls to act as paid monitors. He made a point of stating that the changes he was introducing for the girls had the full approval of the matron. He appealed to members of the Committee to interest themselves in the children's progress and to show this interest by constant inspection and examination.

Discipline

The discipline of the school had two major defects. First, there had been insufficient regard for the characters of the boys and young men, which created distrust and dislike, destroyed confidence and 'blunted better feelings'. Secondly, he disapproved strongly of the 'continual resort to measures of violence and personal chastisement'. His personal view was that

punishment lightly and hastily inflicted on uncertain and changeful rules has always the effect of making its power and moral influence less felt – the just and the unjust inflictions are mingled together – and the offender becomes in his own and his companions' estimation, more or less a martyr. To make a penalty effectual it must be inflicted with discrimination as to the disposition and nature of the criminal and must be inflicted with every possible appearance of firm and serious consideration and there must be kindness and personal attention given when the offence has been punished to make the distinction evident between the offender and his fault – on any other system the punishment, especially if an act of personal violence, must have the effect of multiplying the offences it would correct.

Turner then described the rules he had made for himself, for the staff and for the children, to create good order and discipline. Concerning himself, he stated that he would study every individual boy, give a fair and full hearing in any conflict and make as few rules as possible. Those that had to be made were to be simple and clearly understood. If he found it necessary to punish a boy, he wanted the sentence and the reasons for it to be made as public as possible. He insisted that it would be necessary to excite a sense of self-respect, pride and dignity in the children, but did not think that this could be done through corporal punishment. He employed extra supervisors so that all dormitories were under constant supervision, appointed a 'chief elder' and 'elders' from the older boys, divided the boys into six classes according to age and behaviour, and introduced differential bedtimes according to age. He allowed the children to play games, to do gardening, and to learn music and singing. He made the schoolmaster his deputy and noted with satisfaction that 'the raising and recognizing and defining the rank and powers of his office have already had the good effect of decreasing the cases in which he was obliged to have resort to force to vindicate his authority for himself'.

Employment

In his analysis of the employment situation, Turner strongly deprecated a Committee decision of December 1840 to apprentice boys to masters outside the institution. He urged the reintroduction of the older system of having the boys apprenticed to masters within the institution because, he said,

. . . I look to the Articles of Apprenticeship as a means of securing the boy against his own caprice and ignorance of life as giving the institution more fully the influence of parent and master over him – and as making the boy's employment a more definite and important matter to him – I believe it to be of great importance to the boys to retain them as far as possible during the period of life from fifteen to twenty.

He warned the Committee of the danger of boys being indentured to masters of indifferent character and stressed the advantage of having older boys as journeymen to instruct and influence the younger boys.

In a final comment he offered an explanation for the difficulties the institution had experienced in earlier years:

... the boisterous and unintellectual tendency attributed so freely to [the boys] might perhaps arise from a system of too strict and violent discipline brought in after a system of too great relaxation – both systems being mistaken in not attending sufficiently to the varieties of individual character in not sufficiently studying the comfort of those under the Society's care and in not giving the occasions and inducements necessary for more quiet pursuits.

The Committee fully endorsed Turner's analysis and supported all his recommendations except his demand to have the boys apprenticed within the institution. On this they were adamant and Turner himself seems to have changed his mind on this issue.[1]

In his second report[2] Turner described an over-all improvement in the institution and turned his attention to the 'Reform' section of the school. He found that over the previous twenty years the Reform had received twice as many delinquent boys as the Manufactury but that the average stay in the Reform was only one year and nine months, which he regarded as too short a period to effect a reformation. The Reform boys were responsible for most of the trouble in the Institution and represented most of the school's failures [re-convictions]. Among the delinquent boys there were two clearly differentiated groups. The first group were essentially good boys who had got into trouble through temptation or bad influence, whilst the second and troublesome group were boys of 'confirmed habits of depravity'. The system under which these boys were kept was a system of discipline which Turner described as one that 'hardly deserves the name'.

[1] In his report for 1847 Turner made the point that '. . . a too long continuance in the Institution placed [a boy] in an artificial condition and unfits him for his natural position in society accustoming to habits which he cannot adhere to in the world and impeding the proper development of the boyish into the manly character.'

[2] Report, December 1842.

Unlike the boys in the Manufactury, boys in the Reform were not permitted to leave it and they could be visited by their parents only once in three months. Their diet was about the same as that of other boys, their dress was different but equally good in quality, their work was restricted to shoemaking and tailoring which was compulsory and unpaid, and their day was divided into five hours at school, five hours at work and all domestic work. The boys were under constant supervision which Turner regarded as a negative measure in that it made it impossible to train a boy to resist temptation, but they were also under constant instruction and in continuous contact with members of staff and this he thought was a positive measure. Under such a system Turner thought the good lads would improve whilst the bad boys would remain untouched.

To improve the situation he suggested far-reaching improvements. All new admissions should go into a first division where they would be classified, the good boys would then go to a second division where they would be given more liberty, and the best of these would be transferred to the Manufactury. The bad boys would remain under the more stringent discipline of the first division and the worst of these would be sent to sea. Food was to be increased for all the boys and they were to be given more active exercise and employment.

At the time of this report the Society could accept only one in every ten applications from magistrates who wanted to place delinquent boys. Turner suggested that the Reform should be rebuilt and enlarged, that admissions should be increased to 25 per annum (instead of 10), giving an average population of 60, and that the Government should be asked for an annual vote to maintain these boys.

The records of the Society do not show whether there was any serious objection to any of Turner's proposals for the Reform, though it seems fairly clear that all his suggestions were accepted apart from the recommendation to rebuild and enlarge this part of the institution in London, for it was about this time that reports were received in England of a new French institution for delinquent boys which promised to be useful and possibly relevant to the needs of the children in this country. In 1846 the Committee asked Turner to go to France and to inspect and report on the Colonie Agricole at Mettray. Turner went with

Thomas Paynter, a member of the Committee and a London police magistrate. They published a detailed report on Mettray in that year to which Turner added an important preface in which he laid down many proposals which were to remain effective for many years.[1] In this report Turner pointed out that Mettray was so carefully adapted to the requirements of the French national character that there could be no question of transplanting such an institution to this country, but he did find in Mettray five proposals which he thought could be used in an English setting (Report, pp. 5–7). These were: first, the employment of trained staff; second, the division of inmates into family groups living in a homely setting; third, to act on boys by persuasion rather than force; fourth, to give boys active outdoor occupations such as gardening and agriculture to '. . . prevent the constant communication and intercourse which could scarcely be avoided when the boys are collected together in sedentary trades' (p. 7); and fifth, to combine the charity of individuals with support and sanction of the government.

Turner then described the requirements of a British boy based on his analysis of the English character. The English political system and the Protestant religion made it necessary to teach the boy to think and to think rightly (p. 8); this involved selecting the right kind of staff to exercise the right kind of influence over the boy. Ultimately principles were more important than staff, but he stressed the need for persons who would be '. . . the parent, influencing by affection, not the officer governing by discipline, to make the asylum not a prison for punishment but a school for education' (pp. 9–10). The next issue was the domestic character of English society, and this Turner thought made it essential to have small units for the boys.

Speaking from experience I would say that I would rather take charge of 500 boys distributed in twenty different families of twenty-five each under twenty ordinary and comparatively uneducated men, than of 200 collected together in one large establishment on the common aggregative system though superintended by the best-trained and most efficient master that could be obtained (pp. 10–11).

Turner was convinced that kindly individual instruction was

[1] *Mettray: Report on the System and Arrangements of 'La Colonie Agricole' at Mettray*, 2nd ed. Revised., London, 1846.

more valuable because it would sink deeper and have a more lasting influence. The third factor in the English character was 'firmness amounting almost to obstinacy' which made it inadvisable to deal with an English boy by force. It made it necessary to 'overcome evil with good. The force of gentleness is never more conspicuous than in dealing with hardened and corrupt children. The rock that force cannot break persuasion has again and again been found to melt' (pp. 11–12). Finally, Turner wanted to take into account the practical turn of the English mind which he thought made English boys susceptible to things but not to names, titles of distinction or prospects of reputation. But positive substantial advantages would be required, and for this he suggested an adapted form of the marks system introduced by Captain Maconochie. The adaptations he suggested were based on his perception of the nature of boys to whom 'the future is comparatively nothing, the present everything', whilst 'the man may live by faith . . . the boy, I fear, must live by sight' (p. 13). His main objection to the system employed at Mettray was a criticism that he had also made earlier of the system he found at the Philanthropic: 'the boys appear a little too much looked after on a system of police and hardly thrown enough upon their own responsibility' (p. 14). He explained this further:

Voluntary, not forced good conduct must be the object we aim at; for this alone will last. If we render the boy dependent on the superintendence and discipline which we subject him to, he will be as but a child needing strings; and when the artificial support which he has been used to leaning upon is necessarily withdrawn on his going forth into the world, he will be liable to fall at every step he takes in life (p. 15).

In spite of the reservations expressed in the Report, both Turner and Paynter were firmly convinced that some kind of agricultural colony would be of considerable advantage and the recommendations they made closely foreshadowed the general organization under which reformatory schools came to be established a few years later.

In 1845 a special committee of the institution made two important changes in the structure of the Philanthropic Society school. It was decided not to admit any girls at all, and to restrict the admission of boys to those who had been convicted of a criminal offence.[1]

The next available report was published in 1848 and in it Turner described the new system. His own function was

to administer the internal government of the Society; to take part in the public services of the Chapel; to observe in concert with the steward the system and conduct of the officers, master, etc., that are employed; and to report upon the same to the Committee, a selected portion of which body met weekly at the Institution (p. 7).

Although non-delinquent boys were no longer admitted, the separate Reform and Manufactury were retained. On admission a boy was placed in the Reform, which had about fifteen inmates. New admissions were under close and constant supervision and were not allowed to leave the grounds. Relatives were permitted to visit occasionally, but only in the presence of a member of the staff. The object of the Reform was to 'soften and improve the boy's disposition; to instruct him thoroughly in the elements of religious truth and to accustom him to the habits of cleanliness, industry and order'. To achieve this, 'kindness, regularity and as much personal association with the master as is practicable are the chief instruments resorted to' (p. 10). Mornings and evenings were devoted to school and the afternoon to work in tailoring or shoemaking. The boys remained in the Reform for about a year, but this period could be shortened.

From the Reform the boy went to the Manufactury, which had accommodation for about a hundred boys but at the time of the Report the Society could not afford to take more than seventy (p. 11). Here the boys were instructed mainly in trades and the most intelligent were taught carpentry. The usual stay

[1] The reasons for this decision are given in Turner's Report for 1847: 'the change in the laws relating to the relief of the poor, compelling the family of the transported or executed criminal to enter the Union House, instead of subsisting by aid of outdoor relief, rendered the number of children of convicts who required the Society's assistance very small; while the Institution of improved Schools in connection with the Union House rendered that assistance much less necessary; and the number of applicants of the class juvenile criminals had increased so much as to more than absorb the whole resources of the charity' (*Reformation of Juvenile Offenders: The Philanthropic*, London, 1848. Footnote to p. 8).

was again about a year, at the end of which the boy was placed out as an apprentice to a craftsman. Extra educational classes were provided for the more intelligent boys and privileges were awarded according to the boy's general industry and conduct. All the boys attended divine service twice on Sundays. The Committee tried as best they could to follow up the careers of boys discharged in England by visiting them, enquiring into their condition and '. . . by assembling them on the anniversaries for the first, second and third years after leaving the Society' (p. 14). Turner reported that, taking the previous thirty years, 'there is good reason to believe that 90 per cent of those discharged had not been re-convicted' (p. 14).

Like many prison chaplains of the period, Turner drew attention to the background of the children admitted to the institution.

It is indeed impossible for anyone to enter minutely into the circumstances of such children as those received in the Philanthropic without being struck with the fact that their offences have been much more the result of their situation and the influence they have been subjected to, than to any personal depravity of will and disposition. It is a rule almost without exception, that the boy has been left untaught and uncared for, has been the subject of much ill-treatment and neglect, that the gentler influence of a mother's care, and the comforts of an honest and happy home, have been unknown to him (p. 21).

Following his visits to Mettray and Parkhurst, Turner, with the approval of the Committee, set out to find a suitable place outside London to turn the institution into an agricultural colony. Many suitable sites had to be abandoned because of the prejudice of local inhabitants against an institution of this nature. The Society records the case of one lady who, on learning that enquiries were being made about a site in the vicinity of her home, offered the Society £1,000 to keep away from her district. This the Society accepted.[1] Eventually a farm at Redhill was decided upon and the decision to transfer the institution from London to Redhill was ratified at a general meeting of subscribers in January 1848. In the following year preliminary work had been completed and the first boys were

[1] *The Royal Philanthropic Society*. Redhill, Surrey, 1788–1953. 'The Story of the School' (pamphlet published by the school), p. 8.

transferred from London to Redhill early in 1849. There were then two houses for boys and staff; this was later increased to five. On 30 April 1849 Prince Albert laid the foundation stone of the chapel.[1]

2 PARKHURST[2]

Parkhurst Prison for Boys was established in 1838 as a result of a recommendation of the Lords Committee of 1835 in which they urged

. . . whether the means might not be found in some unoccupied barracks or fort connected with, or in the neighbourhood of, the places of embarkation, of providing for the accomplishment of an object so important as the due custody, the effective punishment and the timely reformation of that large class of juvenile offenders whom the ingenuity of more mature and experienced delinquents renders the instruments of so much and such increasing criminality.[3]

Although Parkhurst was not the first establishment especially set aside by the government for the detention and treatment of young offenders,[4] it was certainly the first government-sponsored institution to do so with any semblance of success. The prison attracted a great deal of attention and hostility, and in spite of the rejection or neglect of this experiment in later years, it was one of the most important in the nineteenth century for three reasons. First, because throughout the twenty-five years of its existence its senior officers and administrators published objective and often highly self-critical annual reports; secondly, because, like the Philanthropic, Parkhurst approached the problems of young offenders in an empirical manner and was flexible enough to change and adapt its

[1] Ibid., p. 9.

[2] A preliminary study of Parkhurst Prison was submitted as a Prize-essay to the I.S.T.D. (London) in 1956. A short article based on this chapter was published in *New Society*, vol. iv, No. 101 (1964), pp. 16–17.

[3] *3rd Report House of Lords Select on the Present State of the Several Gaols and Houses of Correction 1835*, p. v.

[4] From 1823 to 1844 there was a special prison hulk for juveniles run by the notorious J. H. Capper (see W. Branch-Johnson, *The English Prison Hulks*, London, 1957, chap. 16, pp. 146–56).

methods to the observed needs of its inmates; and, thirdly, by becoming the focus of a tremendous amount of hostility from voluntary reformers, Parkhurst inspired a great deal of constructive thinking and writing about the needs of young offenders.

Unlike the Philanthropic, the founders of Parkhurst had a very clear conception of the functions the institution was to serve. The preamble to the Act[1] stated that 'it may be of great public advantage that a prison be provided in which young offenders may be detained and corrected'. Admissions were to be young offenders, male or female, under sentence of transportation or imprisonment. Offenders who proved to be too difficult were to be returned to ordinary prisons to serve their sentences. Three or more 'fit and discreet persons' were to visit at least once a month to enquire into the behaviour and conditions of the prisoners. The Parkhurst Act gave official recognition for the first time to voluntary reformatories by offering a conditional pardon to selected cases to go to charitable institutions for the reception and reformation of young offenders.[2]

In their first report the visitors defined their objectives as follows. First, that the penal correction provided at Parkhurst should be a deterrent not only to the offender but also to juvenile offenders generally. They suggested that 'the utmost care must be taken to avoid any species of discipline which is inconsistent with the habits and character of youth or calculated in any degree to harden and degrade'. Second, to provide 'a judicious course of moral, religious and industrial training; but the means adopted for this purpose should not be of such a nature as to counteract the wholesome restraints of corrective discipline'. Third, that 'every comfort and indulgence' which was not essential to preserve health of mind and body should be excluded and that there should be nothing in the arrangements of the prison which might tend to 'weaken the terror of the law or to lessen in the minds of the juvenile population at large, or of their parents, the dread of being committed to a prison'.[3]

[1] 1 & 2 Vic., p. 82.
[2] Section 11. These cases were chosen by Inspectors of Prisons and sent to the Philanthropic.
[3] *1st Report Relating to Parkhurst Prison*, 1839, p. 1.

On 26 December 1838, 102 boys arrived in Parkhurst drawn from hulks and metropolitan prisons and serving sentences varying from two years' imprisonment to fifteen years' transportation for offences against property. The prison staff were a governor (Robert Woolcombe), chaplain, surgeon, steward, taskmasters, warders, schoolmasters, porters and watchmen. Lord Yarborough, Capt. Jebb, William Crawford and J. P. Kay were the first 'visitors'.

'The Penal Discipline', reported the governor, 'consists of deprivation of liberty, wearing an iron on the leg, a strongly marked prison dress, a diet reduced to its minimum, the enforcement of silence on all occasions of instruction and duty and an uninterrupted surveillance by officers.'[1] But already in February 1839 the Home Office had instructed the governor that leg-irons could be removed for good conduct, and in September 1840 leg-irons were abolished altogether.[2] While the chaplain endeavoured to discover what type of boy found his way into prison, the governor set out to discover some principles which might be applied in the management of his institution. He divided his charges into:

1 Probationary class. Boys were not permitted 'that intercourse with each other which is inseparable from youthful exercise'. Whilst in this class a boy's 'capabilities and habits are noted and he is treated accordingly'.
2 Ordinary class. Boys in this class were not subject to corporal punishment.
3 Refractory class. Received very rough treatment.[3]

It was not long before the governor discovered that 'the constant infliction of summary punishment, which, however great its severity may be, is soon at an end, frequently irritates the worst passions and produces, at the best, but a surly acquiescence'.[4] A second principle was laid down when he decided that 'no labour of any kind is ever imposed on the prisoners as a punishment'.[5]

The chaplain reported that, though the majority of the boys had attended school (in 1840, out of 273 boys admitted, only 13 had never attended a school), the majority could barely read or

---

[1] *Report relating to Parkhurst*, 1840, p. 4.   [2] Ibid., p. 7.
[3] *Report* 1841, p. 4.   [4] Ibid., p. 5.   [5] Ibid., p. 10.

write. The surgeon expressed concern about the diet which consisted almost exclusively of starchy foods.[1] By 1842, numbers in the prison were growing so rapidly that new constructions were begun and additional staff drafted to the prison. Boys were working mostly indoors. The first groups of boys were being send on conditional pardon to Western Australia where they were apprenticed to settlers. But the boys were restless, the treatment uncertain, and the results doubtful. A few boys attempted to escape each year and the numbers in the Refractory Ward increased. In spite of solitary confinement, bread and water, extra drill and whipping, some boys proved too tough to handle and were either transported as convicts or returned to ordinary prisons.

The next stage of the 'Parkhurst Experiment' began with the arrival on 23 August 1843 of Capt. George Hall, an unusual and outstanding officer. His chief warder (later deputy governor) was Mr. Shirlaw, an ex-battalion sergeant major, who worked quietly but most effectively with his Governor.[2] There were at that time 423 boys in Parkhurst and as a first step the new Governor increased the boys' rations and added a daily issue of meat, which rapidly improved the health of the prisoners.[3] The daily routine was re-organized and made a little easier. The prison was now divided into:

1 The General Ward for boys 14 and over.
2 The Junior Ward for boys below 14.
3 The Probationary Ward for boys for the first four months after admission.
4 The Refractory Ward for punishment.
5 The Infirmary Ward for boys needing in-patient treatment.[4]

The Probationary Ward was destined to attract much public attention, for here the boys were kept in separate confinement. Complete isolation was undergone for two months, after which boys mixed during the day. Where the new admissions were very young or weak they were admitted straight into the Junior Ward without undergoing separate confinement in the Probationary Ward.[5]

The boys were working an average of seven hours per day. In

[1] *Report* 1841, p. 40.   [2] *Report* 1844, p. 3.   [3] Ibid., p. 5.
[4] *Report* 1845, pp. 5 and 22.   [5] *Report* 1846, p. 4.

1845, the Home Office, by way of an experiment (which did not prove successful), ordered that all boys should spend one day a week in cells with light employment to give them an opportunity for 'reflection'.[1] The chaplain prepared full records of 'the condition of his [each boy's] parents and relatives, his scholastic and religious acquirements, his habits, associates, etc., and the probable period of his criminality, his conduct under confinement and his improvement, if any.'[2] Hall authorized a pond to be built in the grounds of the prison where boys were permitted to go swimming once every two weeks.[3] Capt. Hall was also searching for fundamental principles which governed the institutional care of delinquents, and his reports contain many ideas which are valid to this day. 'The degrees of progress,' he wrote in 1846, 'may be scarcely perceptible to those whose attention is uninterruptedly directed, day after day, to the observation of conduct.'[4] His first important suggestion is contained in the same report:

The desire to get their liberty by removal to the Colonies for good conduct has a very strong influence over the prisoners here. It appears to me that it would be of advantage to introduce some distinguishing mark or privilege which might be acquired by a prisoner at an earlier period of his confinement and which, being known as a recognition on the part of the Prison Authorities of good conduct so far, should operate as an encouragement and stimulus to the boy to persevere in the course of well-doing, which will eventually procure him a recommendation for liberty.[5]

Whilst Capt. Hall took pride in the excellent reports he received about former Parkhurst boys in Western Australia, he was troubled about the restless inmates who threatened to spoil the over-all tone of the establishment. Prisoners were at this time working mainly indoors and almost half their time was spent in classrooms. To boys unused to so scholarly and sedentary an existence this was bound to be irritating. He advised his visitors that 'the physical and moral advantages of giving to the prisoners healthful and interesting employment in the open air and training them to handicrafts whereby they may readily earn for themselves a comfortable subsistence in the Colonies, are too obvious'.[6]

[1] Ibid., p. 5.   [2] Ibid., p. 10.   [3] Ibid., p. 26.   [4] Ibid., p. 4.
[5] Report 1846, pp. 4–5.   [6] Report 1848, p. 6.

As visitor, Capt. Jebb now had as his colleagues Capt. O'Brien, who undertook the immediate superintendence of Parkhurst, and Mr. Joules. In their report for 1849 they expressed dissatisfaction with the general progress in the prison. They introduced a number of changes including previous suggestions of the Governor, which greatly changed the approach to the management of the boys:

1 Boys were to be graded into first-, second- and third-class prisoners.
2 Schooling was to be cut and emphasis was to be placed on outdoor industrial (e.g., agricultural) training.[1]

A further determined effort was made to establish a system of treatment that could cater for even the most difficult boys. Not only the inmates, but the staff too, were rigorously controlled to satisfy the high standards set by Capt. Hall. In 1850, four officers were dismissed for misconduct. Their dismissal may possibly have been connected with two serious incidents which occurred in that year. In the first, five boys set fire to a ward dormitory in which 158 cells were destroyed. Later in the year some of the younger boys also attempted to set fire to their quarters, but this time unsuccessfully. The prison visitors furnished an interesting description of their charges. 'As a class, boys sent to Parkhurst are very difficult to manage. Many of them, besides having been brought up in idleness, profligacy and vice, are, on their reception, very wilful and impatient of restraint. Their perceptions are singularly acute, whilst their reason is immature or perverted.'[2] Boys were doing everything that was required for prison use. They made and laundered their clothes and footwear, they baked and cooked and undertook all maintenance work. Every prisoner was required to do forty hours' work and to have eleven hours' school per week, excluding Sunday School.

Parkhurst was subjected to much newspaper criticism because in 1849 the largest number ever (34 boys) attempted to escape from the prison when they first began to work outside the prison walls. In order to allay public anxiety, a small military guard

[1] *Report* 1850, pp. 7–8.
[2] *Report of the Directors of Convict Prisons on the Discipline and Management of Parkhurst Prison* 1851, p. 9.

was provided in February 1850 in order to check escapes from the farm.[1]

Like Turner, the chaplain was 'convinced that, were it not for this circumstance [unsatisfactory or non-existent homes] many of these boys would not have been criminals at all; and such as these are, in my estimation, the objects rather of pity than of blame'.[2] The surgeon pointed out

that the inmates of this prison have most of them, previous to their admission, lived in extreme irregularity and young as they are have been in the habit of drinking to excess when they have had the means to gratify their inclinations; that they have been badly clothed, wretchedly lodged and accustomed to the practice of almost every vice.[3]

The boys were settling down to their new tasks and the class system was showing good results. Prisoners received gratuities for work done well on the following scale:

	General ward per week	Junior ward per week
First-class prisoners	6d	4d
Second-class prisoners	3d	2d

Further incentives to good behaviour were added. Perhaps the most important was the special privilege of corresponding with relatives and friends once every three months. Of this the chaplain wrote: 'The reward which is most prized is the liberty of writing to their friends.'[4] Boys who were not entitled to this privilege had to seek a special interview with the Governor to obtain news 'from home'. 'Another incentive', added the visitors somewhat cynically, 'to good conduct, has had a very marked effect. Persons who have been in the habit of dealing with boys will not require to be informed how greatly they prize any gratification, however small, that is connected with eating.' Accordingly, boys in the first and second class received each Sunday 'a ration of pudding in addition to their ordinary diet'.[5]

[1] Ibid., p. 13. The guard consisted of two N.C.O.s and ten men who patrolled the boundaries of the eighty acres that were farmed but did *not* supervise the boys (Capt. Hall's evidence, House of Commons Committee on *Criminal and Destitute Juveniles.* Q.2591, p. 262, and Q.2784, p. 271).
[2] *Report* 1851, p. 15. [3] Ibid., p. 33. [4] Ibid., p. 68. [5] Ibid., p. 52.

The result of encouraging and rewarding, instead of merely controlling, the boys was very marked.

Year	No. of boys	No. of boys punished for offences against rules
1848	455	3,438
1849	545	3,248
1850	526	2,069[1]

Capt. Hall now made a most important change. By keeping the same warders for respective sections he found he could stabilize the groups. He therefore divided his boys as follows:

General Ward: 6 sections (38–42 boys per section)
Junior Ward: 4 sections (50 boys per section)

Each section was in the charge of a warder with one assistant warder.[2] Chaplain Smith found in that year (1851) that, of 154 new boys:

62 had both parents
30 were orphans
62 had one parent only,

and he remarked: 'If industrial orphan schools were established, a vast amount of crime would be prevented and a great expense saved to the country.'[3] Like his predecessor, he found that between 85 and 90 per cent of the boys had attended schools for from six months to seven years, but with very negative results. He observed that 'we seldom get a prisoner from a rural and scattered population' and that 'the remote cause [of delinquency] was a want of proper parental control'.[4] He also studied the background of his boys and reported that most of the boys had many previous convictions.

No. of boys	Previous convictions
14	None
27	1
23	2
24	3
15	4
12	5

[1] Report 1852, p. 61.   [2] Ibid., p. 55.   [3] Ibid., p. 65.   [4] Ibid., p. 66.

No. of boys	Previous convictions
10	6
7	7
2	8
1	9
3	10
3	12
1	14
1	15
3	18
8	Not known

He commented, 'how very much more economical it would be to prevent juvenile crime by an industrial and religious training than, after allowing it to be manufactured and perpetrated, to reform it'.[1] The junior chaplain supported this: 'These poor boys have committed crime under circumstances and temptations which few, perhaps, similarly situated, would have resisted.'[2] Surgeon Dabbs requested in his report that flannel waistcoats with sleeves be added to the boys' winter clothing. His request was granted immediately but had some unexpected repercussions.[3]

In the following year the visitors offered an interesting comment: 'Several of [the boys] have been made, by early ill-treatment, extremely stubborn or irritable, which renders them difficult to be managed'.[4]

Capt. Hall now introduced a scheme whereby boys in the probationary wards would have opportunity to talk to each other and found that this had 'a salutary effect in preparing prisoners for steady and orderly conduct'.[5] Chaplain Smith allowed himself what is almost an outcry:

The tales of pity I hear from these poor orphans are such as would rend any heart and such as sometimes makes me indignant that affluent England which, with so much generosity, cares for foreign distress, should leave these helpless ones to grow up in ignorance and sin, to thieve for their bread and at last to be stamped with the brand of a convict . . . [and he repeated that] the training required to prevent juvenile delinquency is the work more of the parents than the schoolmaster. The downward road to juvenile delinquency [he

[1] Ibid., p. 67.   [2] Ibid., p. 76.   [3] Ibid., p. 85.
[4] Report 1853, p. 54.   [5] Ibid., p. 60.

said] is soon described. In those cases where the parents are living, the first step is through their neglect. The next is idling in the streets; then entering the Public Houses, those curses of our country, after that theatres and places of low amusement.[1]

When the discharge of boys on tickets of leave to the Colonies was discontinued in 1853 it naturally made the boys restless. An alternative system was therefore introduced in the following year, by which a boy could earn his release on licence as follows:

> On arrival:

Probationary Ward	4 months
In Third Class	4 months
In Second Class	6 months
In First Class	
2nd Division	6 months
In First Class	
1st Division	9 months[2]

During the last period a boy could then be recommended for release on licence but

when it is decided that a prisoner shall be recommended for his discharge inquiries are made as to the likelihood of his obtaining employment either among his own friends and relatives, or among such persons as the superior officers of the prison may have induced to befriend him. In the meantime, they are not removed from the other prisoners but they cease to be so rigorously watched as heretofore; they are given the ordinary garments of a working man and though they attend all prison duties they make one step towards the freedom which they are again about to experience.[3]

By 1856 voluntary reformatories were springing up all over the country. 130 boys arrived in Parkhurst who, unlike previous admissions, had not been sentenced to transportation or penal servitude, but to twelve months' or more ordinary imprisonment. 'I foresee', wrote the Governor, 'that it will be vain to expect that the training of this institution can be made effectual during so short a period', and he lamented that, since many such cases would be re-convicted, the blame would be put, unfairly, on Parkhurst.[4] He pleaded strongly for after-care provisions to

---

[1] *Report* 1853, pp. 62–63.   [2] *Report* 1855, pp. 52–53.   [3] Ibid., p. 53.
[4] *Report* 1857, pp. 97–98.

be made, including provision for suitable employment.[1] In the following year Capt. Hall remarked that 'the privation of hope has a strong tendency to induce reckless and despondent carelessness with regard to conduct', and he therefore recommended remission of sentence for good conduct.[2] The creation of voluntary reformatories had another effect: 'The boys now sent to Parkhurst are almost all of the very worst character, the reformatory establishments throughout the country receiving the better class.'[3] By 1859, 75 per cent of all admissions were short-sentence cases and 25 per cent were under sentence of penal servitude. Governor Hall again pleaded for after-care arrangements.[4] Numbers were falling considerably and by 1860 they were the lowest since 1844. Almost as if to console himself, Capt. Hall described, with considerable satisfaction, the visits and letters he received from former inmates of Parkhurst. Chaplain Warleigh's reports are by now a little less astute, at times even rambling. 'It is most cheering to go as I do, time after time, to visit in the Refractory Ward and to find it empty. I have known the time when it was rarely empty, but often full; now it is never full, almost always without an inmate and seldom above one or two at a time.'[5] But he still had useful comments:

In almost all cases, criminality began after leaving school and in the streets and mostly at nights. Now, for the most part, these poor boys have but few attractions at home and it appears to me that if night schools could be established for them or some other places of recreation, improvement and innocent amusement, most of these boys would gladly avail themselves of them; and that thereby much crime and sin would be prevented.[6]

By 1861 numbers were down to 239 and the Junior Ward was closed. Sixteen officers were discharged, Chaplain Smith-Warleigh was retired. J. J. Spear became the sole chaplain. Surgeon Dabbs too was discharged as it was felt that a full-time resident medical officer was superfluous.[7] The fall in numbers continued and in 1862 a further seven officers were discharged or transferred. Capt. Hall repeated an old complaint: 'It has

---

[1] Ibid., p. 100.   [2] *Report* 1858, p. 93.   [3] Ibid., p. 101.
[4] *Report* 1860, pp. 90–91.   [5] *Report* 1861, p. 101.   [6] Ibid., pp. 101–102.
[7] *Report* 1862, pp. 99–100.

been very distressing to me to be quite unable to respond effectively to the appeals of young men and boys about to be discharged from Parkhurst, who have begged me to find them some place of employment.'[1] This time he was strongly supported by the Directors: 'Until there shall be more organized and satisfactory means of disposal for discharged juvenile convicts, much of the good effect which might be confidently relied upon as a result of discipline and industrial training will be sacrificed.'[2]

When Sir Joshua Jebb died suddenly in 1863 a new group of directors, with little apparent sympathy for Parkhurst, took over. E. Y. W. Henderson was the new Chairman, and with him served I. M. Gambier, E. Du Cane and W. Fagan. All vacant cells in Parkhurst were occupied by female convicts, and for one year Capt. Hall shared his institution with them.[3] He presented no further reports. The boys' section of Parkhurst was closed in April 1864 when the last seventy-eight inmates were escorted to Dartmoor by Capt. Hall who was then retired.

3 LESSONS OF THE PROTOTYPAL INSTITUTIONS

There is little in the general field of residential treatment of young offenders that was not brought out, recorded and discussed by those responsible for the Philanthropic and for Parkhurst. The main issues which were and which remain so crucial can be reviewed under five headings.

(i) *Admissions*

Both institutions quickly realized the importance of defining and classifying the type of youngster who was to be admitted, and the chaos that is likely to result if categories of admission are too wide. The first classification with which both institutions were concerned are what Mannheim and Spencer have called 'external'.[4] The Philanthropic first rejected delinquent girls, then girls altogether, then boys who were not offenders, boys

---

[1] *Report* 1862, p. 102.   [2] Ibid., p. 99.   [3] *Report* 1864, p. 85.

[4] H. Mannheim and J. C. Spencer, *Problems of Classification in the English Penal and Reformatory System*, London, 1953, I.S.T.D., p. 1.

who were too young and boys who were too old. Parkhurst, although legally entitled to do so, never accepted girls at all and became increasingly reluctant to accept boys under ten and boys of eighteen. Both institutions became more and more specific in the type of young offender they wanted. The Philanthropic was to some extent protected here, because they had a right to refuse admissions, but the Parkhurst system broke down altogether when they received an indiscriminate conglomeration of long-term and short-term prisoners.

The second type of classification was related to the structure of the institution itself. At the Philanthropic the Manufactury dealt with the younger and less serious offender, and the Reform with a somewhat stricter discipline, took the older and more hardened young criminal. This same division took place in Parkhurst where the younger and weaker lad was admitted to the junior wards, whilst the older and more difficult boy was placed in the general ward.[1] Both Turner and Hall had fully grasped the importance of reducing large numbers into small units by dividing their institutions into houses in the Philanthropic and wards at Parkhurst.

The third form of classification relates to the personalities and backgrounds of individual offenders. In both institutions the senior officers learned to make a clear distinction between two main groups, each of which had a sub-group. On the one hand they described the youngster whose delinquency is related mainly to his social background, who is in need of training rather than re-training and who is more in need of kindness, affection and security than discipline and correction. On the other hand was the usually older, tougher, more hardened young criminal who was both emotionally and intellectually dedicated to some extent to a criminal way of life and who stood in need not only of reform but also of a vigorous demonstration of the power of the law. In both these groups Turner and Hall found sub-groups of physically, emotionally or intellectually handicapped youngsters who were either too weak and delicate to undergo a normal training process, or needed a

[1] Although the Junior Ward was supposed to cater for boys under fourteen, transfers were made more by size and general maturity than age. In practice, boys were often sixteen at transfer (Capt. Hall: Committee on *Criminal and Destitute Juveniles*, 1852, Q.2598–2601, p. 262).

very specialized form of care to adjust to their handicaps, or were so difficult that they could not be dealt with in the context of an ordinary training institution.

(ii) *Programme*

The training programmes of both institutions underwent considerable changes at two levels. In the case of discipline, both institutions learned that harsh and unreasonable subjugation of young boys never achieved its object. Both institutions adjusted their treatment by improving the food, reducing the scale and frequencies of punishments, by providing scaled incentives to good behaviour (rewards) and by permitting their charges to make and maintain contact with their homes. In the field of training, both institutions moved away from punitive labour and the exploitation of inmates as a cheap labour force, and introduced instead industrial training programmes geared to employment opportunities and post-discharge careers of the boys.

(iii) *Staff*

Turner and Hall were both concerned with the problems of recruiting and training the right kind of staff, and the difficulties in trying to overcome the disparity between low-salaried, poorly-qualified officers, and good officers who could only be obtained by providing a good salary. In both institutions attempts were made to define the functions of each level of authority, and the relationship between the definition and exercise of function was stated explicitly. In both institutions it was fully recognized that the ultimate instrument of reformation is the quality of the relationship between staff and inmates, and both described their awareness of the important principle that the behaviour of inmates is in a large measure a reflection of the attitudes and integrity of the officers.

(iv) *Discharge (After-care)*

Both institutions realized quickly and stressed consistently that even the best type of boy discharged from the institution would be likely to revert to criminal behaviour if he were permitted to return to his original background without some kind of positive supervision and control, and without adequate preparations for the right kind of employment under a suitable, and to some extent, protective employer. Both men regarded emigration as the ideal solution to this problem but thought that a discharge in England could be made feasible provided the youngster was not left entirely to his own devices once the institution had relinquished physical control over him.

(v) *Organization*

The two institutions differed in the way administrative power was focused. In the Philanthropic, Turner assumed full control and became policy-maker and spokesman for the school. His committee acted as a supportive rather than a controlling body. In Parkhurst, the military background of Jebb and Hall determined the pattern. Jebb formulated policy and assumed responsibility for it to Parliament even though many of his reforms arose directly from Hall's recommendations.

4 PARKHURST AND ITS CRITICS

First reactions to the newly established Parkhurst Prison for Boys were suspicion and doubt. As yet, no government institution had been established of which those likely to take an interest in penal reform could think very highly. Both local and central prisons were still in a state of almost total chaos and the little that was known about Capper and the prison hulk for juveniles which he managed was hardly likely to inspire confidence in the ability of the government to set up a satisfactory institution. Public feeling cannot have been reassured by the early reports on Parkhurst which were published by the Visitors and senior officers. The discipline at the prison was repressive, yet, there were recurring admissions that the boys remained hostile and unreformed. Although there was a steady improvement, especially after the arrival of Capt. Hall, many influential people who visited the prison were not impressed. There was a further difficulty in that the plan and intention of the Parkhurst Act was handicapped because Parkhurst and its objectives were unique in the British penal system and could not expect administrative co-operation from other penal institutions. For example, the main source of supply for Parkhurst was Millbank Prison which assembled boys from local gaols all over the country and passed them on. These boys lived in one room in Millbank, which served as dormitory and workshop, under appalling conditions, so that by the time they arrived at Parkhurst the task of reforming them had been made infinitely more difficult. The average time each boy spent in Millbank was fourteen months.[1] Although the reorganization of Parkhurst in 1849 was altogether beneficial, it led to one issue which has been kept alive to this day. As we have seen, when the boys were first taken out for farm work thirty-four attempted to escape and the local residents were in uproar. To prevent a repetition of this and to allay public anxiety, a small military guard was introduced in 1850 to keep an eye on boys working on the farms. Although this guard remained for no more than four years,[2] it, together with the chains used in the first two years, became the symbols of Parkhurst for all twentieth-century writers.

The history of Parkhurst and its role in the provisions for young offenders might have been very different if it had not been for Mary Carpenter, a brilliant, volatile, passionate and arrogant woman whose life, work and prejudices were to dominate the history of the management of juvenile delinquency.

Mary Carpenter's hostility to Parkhurst obscured two main questions which were being debated. Since the mid-1840s it had been suggested that the care and training of delinquent children should be undertaken by the government.[3] Spokesmen for the Voluntary Reform Movement were opposed to this in principle,[4] but the issue was never properly debated and the final

---

[1] *Report of Commissioners on the Management of Millbank Prison*, 1847, p. 362. The same kind of handicap interfered with discharges. Boys sometimes had to wait for months to get a ship to Australia (Committee on *Criminal and Destitute Juveniles*, 1852, Q.2621, p. 263).

[2] When Mary Carpenter visited Parkhurst in August 1854 the guard had been withdrawn (J. E. Carpenter: *The Life and Work of Mary Carpenter*, London, 1881, p. 160).

[3] Cf. Charles Pearson in *The Times*, 16 February 1846.

[4] Cf. Rev. W. L. Clay: 'Act of Parliament philanthropy is no match for volunteer benevolence' in the *Prison Chaplain: A Memoir of the Rev. John Clay*, London, 1861.

word on the subject was not pronounced until the Gladstone Committee Report (1895), which pointed out that, desirable as the voluntary principle was, the control of institutions for young offenders by the government was essentially a good thing. They pointed to the reformatories and industrial schools as an example of State-controlled, yet successful, institutions. The second and very much more important problem concerned the question of whether or not prison was a suitable place for children. Mary Carpenter's opposition led to a failure of a definition of terms on which much of the subsequent confusion was based. There was, for example, universal agreement as far as young children were concerned. Prison was not the proper place for them. That there might well be a useful function for prison in dealing with older and more hardened offenders was readily agreed by many of those who ardently supported Mary Carpenter. But there was no such agreement about the function of imprisonment. Northcote thought that Mary Carpenter's rejection of prison treatment could only be justified on the assumption that a prison was a place for punishment and that its purpose was to deter those outside the prison. On such a definition, prison could not be a place of reformation.[1] Harriet Martineau took a very different view. She did not think that either retribution or deterrence were legitimate aims of imprisonment. She regarded prison as the proper place for the reformation of adult offenders but rejected it as unsuitable for children on the grounds that it mixed tried and convicted, young and old, sophisticated and innocent offenders, that it tended to train the young towards more efficient criminality, that it branded the child for life as a convict and that, if the prison attempted to overcome these handicaps by the use of separate confinement, this too would be undesirable because separate confinement was too cruel a form of treatment to subject children to.[2]

John Clay did not reject prison outright, even for young offenders. He claimed to have introduced a modified system of separate confinement which was effective for some young

---

[1] Sir S. Northcote, 'Reformatory Schools', *Quarterly Review*, December 1855, pp. 32–65.
[2] 'The Management and Disposal of our Convict Population', *Edinburgh Review*, October 1854, pp. 563–632.

Dc

offenders. He described these as boys who had momentarily gone astray but had good homes to return to. He agreed, however, that such prison discipline would only be effective during a short sentence. Young offenders in need of long-term training who came from bad homes, he thought, should go to a reformatory school.[1] Jebb and his associates also disliked the idea of sending young offenders to prison but felt that for the older boys, particularly those who would prove too difficult for a reformatory, prison treatment was the best solution.[2]

It has already been shown that to men like Turner, Jebb and Hall, the problem of delinquency was a relatively simple one. They thought that causation and therefore prevention of delinquency lay in the social conditions of the lower classes from which the delinquents were drawn. None of her contemporaries paid much attention to one of Mary Carpenter's most important contributions in this field, for she took a very different view of the problem of delinquency. According to Mary Carpenter, any child of any social class could be expected to commit delinquent acts of some kind. The difference between the upper and the lower social classes lay in the fact that whereas the upper class child that was guilty of a delinquent act was corrected, restrained and trained through that act by its parents in an over-all framework of love and kindness, the lower class child faced one of two dangers. Either its delinquent act went undetected and untreated and thereby acted as a corrupting force on the child, which, by a process of repetition would ultimately turn the child into a professional criminal, or the child was detected in its delinquent act and by being put through the penal processes as if it were an adult, was corrupted by that process towards the same form of professional criminality. She argued that both in the treatment and the prevention of juvenile delinquency the essential thing was to treat a child in the right way rather than in a legally or socially acceptable

[1] J. Clay, *Chaplain's 30th and 31st Reports on the County Houses of Correction of Preston presented to the Magistrates of Lancashire*, Preston, 1855, pp. 72 and 86.

[2] In his Report on the *Discipline and Management of the Convict Prisons for 1851* (publ. 1852) Jebb argued that, though 'mere children of 12 or 13 years old should not be held very seriously responsible for their acts' (p. 99), there were some older ones who needed a specifically penal system which a reformatory could not provide (p. 103).

way.[1] This emphasis on the need to look at the child of any social class as having needs arising from its developmental processes might have changed and improved the general outlook on the treatment of young offenders if Mary Carpenter had not allowed herself to be deflected by her battle against the English directors of convict prisons.

Apart from the general debates on the value of voluntary management and of imprisonment, there was the reaction to the Parkhurst experiment itself. As far as the contemporaries of that prison (and of Mary Carpenter) were concerned, they were by no means all equally hostile, though the expression of their views was sometimes tempered by a fear of offending the leaders of the voluntary reformatory school movement. Turner visited Parkhurst after he had seen Mettray. Although he seemed to be quite satisfied with what he saw, he never stated this publicly.[2] Lord Norton visited Parkhurst very shortly after it was opened, accompanied by the Home Secretary. He offered some explanation for the severe discipline in use in Parkhurst in its early years. During the visit the prison governor appealed for a pardon[3] for a boy of eight, but the Home Secretary refused because of the 'suspicion in the public mind of the first advances at Parkhurst towards a better treatment of the young outcasts of society'.[4]

Baker had always maintained that there should be a place like Parkhurst where the more difficult young criminal could be detained.[5] Not even Harriet Martineau accepted Mary Carpenter's strictures, for all her support of the reformatory school movement. She appears to have thought highly of

[1] Cf. *Reformatory Schools*, Chapter I, 'Condition of Children – Principles of Schools for them'; and *Juvenile Delinquents*, Chapter IX, 'Principles of Treatment'.

[2] In the resident chaplain's journal, Turner made the following entry on 7 December 1846: 'The Chaplain returned late last night from Parkhurst. The results of his examination of that establishment are very satisfactory . . . the junior school being in all respects an admirable institution. In the senior department there is more penal and military discipline – less education.'

[3] Under Section 11 of the Parkhurst Act.

[4] W. S. Childe-Pemberton: *Life of Lord Norton* (C. Adderley, M.P.), 1814–1905, London, J. Murray, 1909, pp. 95–96.

[5] L. T. B. Baker, in *War with Crime*, edited by H. Phillips and E. Verney, London, 1889, p. 184.

Joshua Jebb and his work as director of convict prisons.[1] Sir Stafford Northcote went even further. He is the only writer of note in this period to challenge seriously Mary Carpenter's criticisms. He rejected her examples of bad behaviour as being far more typical of youngsters in any kind of institution than of a useless prison regime. He went so far as to suggest of some of the things done in reformatories that, if they had originated in Parkhurst, they would have led to a public outcry.[2] Joseph Adshead also disregarded Mary Carpenter's work but described Parkhurst as unsuitable because of what he called 'the outlet question'. He saw correctly that the discharge and disposal methods available to Parkhurst made it unlikely that it would succeed.[3]

Following the closure of Parkhurst, with the reformatories firmly and widely established, the debate ceased for a while, but it became increasingly obvious that the reformatories were unable to cope with those young offenders who were most hardened in crime and therefore most dangerous to society. A demand arose for the establishment of penal reformatories and in this context Parkhurst was frequently quoted as an example.[4] It came up again and again until the demand was finally met by the Gladstone Committee which, whilst accepting the need for a measure halfway between a reformatory and a prison, displayed a curious reluctance to look at Parkhurst. They asked Du Cane why Parkhurst had been a failure and he denied that it had.[5] They asked Capt. Hill the same question and he replied

[1] *Edinburgh Review*, October 1854, pp. 563–632 and April 1855, pp. 383–415.

[2] *Quarterly Review*, December 1855, pp. 32–65.

[3] J. Adshead, *Juvenile Criminals*, 'Reformatories and the Means of Rendering the Perishing and Dangerous Classes Serviceable to the State', Manchester, 1856, p. 26.

[4] See, for example, A. King in a paper on Reformatory Extension read at the *5th Conference of the National Association of Certified Reformatory and Industrial Schools*, Birmingham, 1891, pp. 54–60. 'At both Parkhurst and Redhill such [older] youths were dealt with and the success of the Reformatory treatment they received compares very favourably with our present work. . . .' See also *25th Report Inspector of Reformatory and Ind. Schools*, 1882, which pointed out that, in the absence of a penal reformatory, incorrigibles are transferred or discharged, p. 6.

[5] *Report of the Departmental Committee on Prisons* 1895. Evidence Qs. 10914–10919, pp. 369–70.

that he had once employed an ex-chief warder from Parkhurst who had told him that there 'the boys got the mastery of them'.[1] On the basis of this 'evidence' the report stated that 'it is almost impossible to ascertain to what extent the Parkhurst Government Reformatory was a success'.[2] The Departmental Committee on Reformatory and Industrial Schools (1896) was better informed on Parkhurst and included in its report an appendix describing some of the work done there and some of the criticisms that prison had to face. But there is a somewhat undue emphasis on early years and conceptions.[3]

With the turn of the century, writers on Parkhurst become uniformly hostile and seem to base their statements on half-truths or false information. This is mainly due to the remarkable influence which Mary Carpenter's books have wielded and are still wielding.

In 1902 a Fabian pamphlet reported that the discipline in Parkhurst 'was very strict and all the inmates wore irons'.[4] Russell and Rigby found that 'although school instruction, outdoor labour and religious teaching were provided, the place remained a thorough prison and its inmates were vicious and were guarded by armed sentinels'.[5] Barnett wrote that boys 'were kept in chains and when at work they were guarded by warders with loaded rifles'.[6] Similarly, Spielman maintained that Parkhurst was closed as a failure in 1864

because it was carried on on prison lines, there was a guard of military sentinels with fixed bayonets, there was the massing of hundreds of vicious youths . . . no voluntary management . . . no individual care . . . nothing was done for their future welfare on discharge and there was no emigration.[7]

Burt described the setting up of Parkhurst prison 'but the young

---

[1] Op. cit., Qs. 7389–7391, p. 254.   [2] Op. cit., *Report*, para. 84, p. 30.

[3] *Report*, para. 8, p. 10, and Appendix II, pp. 181–3.

[4] H. T. Holmes, *Reform of Reformatories*, Fabian Tract No. 111, London, 1902, p. 2.

[5] C. E. B. Russell and L. M. Rigby, *The Making of the Criminal*, London, 1906, pp. 207–8.

[6] Mary G. Barnett, *Young Delinquents*, A Study of Reformatory and Industrial Schools, London, 1913, p. 18.

[7] M. A. Spielman, *The Romance of Child Reclamation*, London, Reformatory and Refuge Union, 1921, pp. 61–2.

inmates were still fettered in chains; and while at work guarded by warders with loaded rifles'.[1] Cadbury, who acknowledged Mary Carpenter as her source of information, also described the 'sentinels with loaded guns' and remarked that Parkhurst was 'finally stopped by the Government with only too good reason'.[2] Mannheim selected a comment on Parkhurst which was made nine years after its establishment, to the Lords Committee in 1847, that 'the establishment of Parkhurst prison had achieved but little in fighting juvenile delinquency', but he ignores the more important developments which took place between 1847 and 1864.[3] Even more surprising are the comments made by Young and Ashton that

Parkhurst was established as a juvenile prison in 1837 with the school as an integral part of it. But as the schools were run by fear, the boys frequently wearing irons when in school and the school-masters were usually themselves convicted felons, it was seldom that they achieved any education or reformation.[4]

5 MARY CARPENTER AND RED LODGE

Mary Carpenter was born in Exeter on 3 April 1807 and was the first child of the Non-Conformist minister, Dr. Lant Carpenter. Even as a child she was a serious and studious person, passionately devoted to her father and to her religion. In her early years her main interests were literary and scientific, and she assisted her father in teaching pupils in his private school. In 1831, when only twenty-four, she became superintendent of a Sunday school and there she first became aware of the problems of the poor, particularly when in that year riots broke out in Bristol where she had lived since she was ten. She was deeply convinced that some great duty was reserved for her and spent

[1] C. Burt, *The Young Delinquent*, London, 4th Edition, reprinted 1961, p. 105.

[2] Geraldine S. Cadbury, *Young Offenders – Yesterday and Today*, London, 1938, pp. 47–8.

[3] H. Mannheim, Previous Investigations in A. M. Carr-Saunders, H. Mannheim, E. C. Rhodes, *Young Offenders – An Enquiry into Juvenile Delinquency*, 1942, p. 5.

[4] A. F. Young and E. T. Ashton, *British Social Work in the 19th Century*, London, 1956, p. 164.

many years in an earnest search to find that field in which God had meant her to be his agent. In 1835 she became secretary of the Working and Visiting Society which had been established by her father for visiting the homes of the poor of the Sunday school. After the death of her father in 1840 she spent some two years in a depressed and anxious state from which she gradually recovered after a Continental journey. She now took a keen interest in the abolition of slavery movement which was spreading from America to England and the plight of the children of the poor continued to engage her active interest. Having studied the results of John Pound's Ragged School Movement and the success of Sheriff Watson's Industrial Feeding School in Scotland, she decided in 1846 to open a Ragged School at Lewin's Mead. The school was highly successful and had to be enlarged in the same year. It was here that Mary Carpenter learned something of the effects of imprisonment on those of her pupils who had already served one or more sentences. When they reappeared in class after a brief term of imprisonment, she found that they entered without shame and were greeted almost respectfully by their fellows. In the following year she acquired the land around her school and turned it into a residential settlement for selected tenants. The study of the 'vagrant and lawless class' around her began to absorb more and more of her interest and she started to correspond with some of the better-known prison chaplains (Carter of Liverpool, Clay of Preston, Osborne of Bath) in order to exchange views. She also contacted Sheriff Watson of Aberdeen and the famous Recorder of Birmingham, Matthew Davenport Hill. After studying the Report of the Select Committee of 1847 she was shocked to find that nothing had been done[1] or was contemplated and decided that there was no way open but to make the facts known and trust that a conscience-stricken public might demand reforms.

In 1851 she wrote and published a book, *Reformatory Schools*,[2] in which she described the extent of juvenile crime and the plight of lower class children. She made a clear differentiation

---

[1] The Committee had recommended the establishment of 'Reformatory Asylums' on the Parkhurst pattern (*2nd Report House of Lords Committee on Juvenile Offenders and Transportation*, 1847, p. 6).

[2] *Reformatory Schools for the Children of the Perishing and Dangerous Classes and for Juvenile Offenders*, London, 1851.

between destitute, neglected and criminal children and suggested free day schools, compulsory industrial feeding schools and reformatory schools as the best method of dealing with these three groups. She urged Mettray, the Rauhe Haus and, to a lesser extent, Redhill, as models of reformatory institutions, and strongly attacked the idea of sending any child to prison, although she agreed that Parkhurst would be a suitable place for the more difficult boy of fifteen and over.[1] To demonstrate the undesirability of prison for the reformation of young offenders, she included in her book a bitter attack on Parkhurst in which she pointed out that, although well organized, it was a 'prison in name and in fact',[2] that in one year alone 34 boys attempted to escape, that 165 were whipped, and that 79 had been returned to Millbank as being incorrigible.[3] She insisted that 'it is utterly vain to look for any real reformation where the heart is not touched' and that this 'cannot possibly be done for children under the mechanical and military discipline of Parkhurst'.[4] She explained her reason for attacking the prison by saying that it was regarded by many as a model institution and that it was therefore necessary to point out the radical defects of the system.[5] It is evident from our table that the figures quoted by Mary Carpenter were highly selective. This technique of extracting items of information which supported her arguments and ignoring the context in which they were provided became characteristic of all her subsequent writing, both in attacking ideas and people which she disliked and in supporting ideas and people she approved of.

Reformatory Schools was an immediate success and attracted the attention of a large number of people who had been conscious of the need for action and who had been waiting for just such a comprehensive and able review of the situation. The response to her book encouraged Mary Carpenter to call a conference of like-minded individuals in December 1851 in Birmingham for the purpose of considering 'the condition and treatment of the Perishing and Dangerous Classes of children and juvenile offenders'[6] and the remedies which their con-

---

[1] Op. cit., p. 315.　　[2] Op. cit., p. 312.　　[3] Op. cit., pp. 319 and 321.
[4] Op. cit., p. 322.　　[5] Ibid.
[6] *Report of the Proceedings of a Conference on Preventive and Reformatory Schools*, London 1851, p. v.

TABLE I

*Figures available to Mary Carpenter when she wrote
'Reformatory Schools'*

Year	Number of boys in Parkhurst	Recorded attempts to escape	Recorded number of whippings
1838	102	5	2
1839	157	6	12
1840	257	5	40
1841	302	—	16
1842	375	6	—
1843	423	4	—
1844	645	—	165 (population increases 50%)
1845	648	10	—
1846	647	3	—
1847	620	3	—
1848	622	20	—
1849	687	34	— (farm work introduced)
1850	516	11	—
1851	558	1	—

dition demanded. The conference did not attract as much attention as had been hoped but did lead to a resolution being laid before the Secretary of State for Home Affairs (Sir George Grey) who told a deputation from that conference that there was not sufficient public interest to warrant legislation.[1] He did, however, agree to appoint a Commission of Enquiry which sat in 1852 and (following the dissolution of Parliament) again in 1853. Mary Carpenter appeared before this Commission on 21 and 25 May 1852. 'I do not believe', she told the Commissioners, 'that reformation is compatible with the general system adopted at Parkhurst'[2] and explained that she had never visited Parkhurst but based her views on the official report for 1849. She agreed that particularly difficult boys should be sent to Parkhurst but denied all knowledge of the major changes which had been introduced in the boys' prison in 1849.[3]

[1] *Report of the Proceedings of the Second Conference*, London 1854, p. 3.
[2] *Committee Criminal and Destitute Juveniles*, 1852. Q.833, p. 102.
[3] Op. cit., Q.1110, p. 140.

Her hostility to Parkhurst, which was so poorly based, did not make a good impression on the Commission. Other workers in the field were preparing draft legislation which planned to include a term of imprisonment prior to admission to reformatories. This plan 'filled her with alarm'[1] and Mary Carpenter decided to establish the undesirability of Parkhurst and the principle of previous imprisonment, once and for all, by writing another book and by starting a reformatory in which she could demonstrate the truth of her principles. Early in 1853 *Juvenile Delinquents* was published[2] which contained another bitter attack on Parkhurst Prison,[3] in which she somewhat dishonestly introduced the story of a boy in Manchester Prison who had committed suicide and in which she spoke of 'those unhappy young persons who have become, to their unspeakable misfortune, the children of the State'. She concluded that Parkhurst was 'most costly, most inefficacious for any end but to prepare the child for a life of crime'.[4]

Joshua Jebb, the Director of Convict Prisons, was basically in agreement with Mary Carpenter. Already, in 1847, he had written that

the whole system hitherto pursued with the respect to youth appears to be open to the most serious objections, both as regards the practice of sentencing mere children to transportation, or committing them to the penal discipline of the prison. The bulk of convicts below the age of thirteen and fourteen are the objects of pity rather than justice.[5]

But the reckless remarks in *Juvenile Delinquents* stung him to a defence of the boys in his care. On 2 March 1853 he wrote to Mary Carpenter:[6]

[1] *Life and Work*, p. 128.
[2] *Juvenile Delinquents – Their Condition and Treatment*, London, 1853. Kingswood Reformatory was opened in 1852.
[3] Op. cit., pp. 192–202.   [4] Op. cit., p. 202.
[5] *2nd Report Surveyor General of Prisons*, 1847, p. 56. See also J. Carlebach, 'Major-General Sir Joshua Jebb 1793–1863', *Prison Service Journal*, Vol. iv, No. 15, 1965, pp. 18–30.
[6] A copy of this letter is in Box 1 of a collection of letters and MSS. of Sir J. Jebb in the Library of the London School of Economics. It has not been published except for a short excerpt in my article in *New Society*.

You are little aware of how greatly the industrious efforts of those who, in pursuit of a favourite theory, have sought to further their ends by creating an unfavourable impression of Parkhurst, have defeated the objects they had in mind of promoting the foundation of industrial establishments.

My duties among the magistracy of the country bring me acquaintance with the obstacles that interfere with progress and improvement in this direction. For years I have urged the union of Counties and Boroughs for the purpose of forming establishments for juvenile criminals as a substitute for ordinary prisons. In some instances I have had a distinct prospect of success, but the whole has vanished on someone asserting that he had it on the most indisputable authority of Mr. —— or Miss —— that Parkhurst had been an entire failure.

This, the only establishment which has been formed for receiving young criminals from prison and making any endeavour to combine the punishment due to crime with a reformatory and industrial training, is held up as a warning against the formation of any such for the future. It has been stated in proof of this failure that boys run away and rob, that they set fire to the prisons, attempt to murder the warders, and crouching with fear all the day long, are only kept in subjection by brute force, that sentries with loaded muskets and fixed bayonets are ready to shoot them and that the entire expense so far as the assumed object is concerned is thrown away.

Now all this may be probably true of several individuals among the hundreds of desperate characters who have passed through Parkhurst within the last twelve or fourteen years, but if anyone argues on the isolated and exceptional cases, the very best and most highly cultivated society in this country may be placed in a light that would be a disgrace to the savage tribes who wander over the wilds of Australia.

It is altogether unfair, and what is worse, being based upon single facts, wholly inapplicable as arguments, it conveys an absolutely false impression.

Such impressions being made, however, is productive of the same results as if it were true. Hence the widespread mischief that will be the consequence of the diligence with which Parkhurst has been vilified.

It will take years of prudent and energetic exertion on the part of those who have been thus engaged to regain what they themselves have lost by such misdirected efforts. They have shaken the confidence of Parkhurst and the public in any such institution and it will not be easy to win it back.

51

One deplorable effect of your exertions in branding a Parkhurst boy before the face of the whole world will be that now, when there is a prospect of a large proportion being released in this country, they will have little or no chance of obtaining employment and may be driven from sheer want and necessity into the criminal career which first brought them within the grasp of the law.

I do not hesitate to say that, looking to the very just influence which you have a right to command, thousands whom you characterize as 'these unhappy young persons who have become to their unspeakable misfortune the children of the State' will have to rue for themselves and for their descendants after them the anathema you have pronounced against them. The moral and industrial training they have received will save many, but the trial of all will be fearfully increased and it is difficult to estimate the amount of misery which will have been entailed upon them.

I am pained thus to address one for whom I have always entertained the most unfeigned respect, with whom I could have so cordially co-operated, but I am impelled by a sense of duty to the officers who have for years devoted their best energies to the promotion of the combined objects of the Government, no less than of justice to the poor boys themselves, to point out to you some of the effects which have resulted, and will inevitably follow, from the course which you and others have adopted.

(Sgd.) J. JEBB

This letter had an unfortunate effect on Mary Carpenter. Already in adolescence she had confessed to her diary 'her unwillingness to own herself in the wrong or to allow herself to be considered in the wrong'.[1] She appealed to Matthew Davenport Hill who advised her to be aggressive in her reply to Jebb, whilst her family counselled silence in the face of this bitter outburst. Worst of all, Jebb's remarks threw her into a deep confusion because they challenged her conviction that what she was doing was the work of God intended for her by God and therefore right. At the same time, Jebb's appeal to her to have some regard 'for the poor boys' seemed to undermine the whole purpose of her existence which she regarded as being exclusively devoted to the protection of children from abuse by others. As if to support Jebb's remarks and his warning that outrageous behaviour might be expected in any institution, the children at

[1] *Life and Work*, p. 12. See also *Frances Power Cobbe: Life* (by herself) London, 1894, pp. 276–7.

Kingswood rioted on 15 March and had to be distributed among the neighbours where they were kept with their hands bound, 'My poor girls and I', wrote Mary Carpenter, 'wept together while I told them ... that they had now compelled us ... to give them up to the magistrates, as we could not control them.'[1] From now on, the question of Parkhurst, of prison management, and of the Directorate of Convict Prisons became a growing obsession with her. In 1854, after visiting Parkhurst at the invitation of Capt. Hall, she was almost embarrassed by being 'led to take a much more favourable view than she had previously expressed'.[2] She wrote to Jebb that although she was not prepared to accept Parkhurst she would make a point of emphasizing the many changes of which she approved, which she had found on her visit. But she did not do so. In the late 1850s the conflict between the English and Irish convict systems which centred on Jebb and Sir Walter Crofton attracted her interest and she became a vigorous defender of the Irish system. Although she had told the Commission on Criminal and Destitute Juveniles in 1852 that she thought the more difficult older adolescent boy should be treated at Parkhurst,[3] she violently rejected this idea when it was suggested once more at a meeting of the National Association for the Promotion of Social Science in 1862. In the presence of Jebb she uttered another vicious attack on Parkhurst in which she repeated that no youngster could ever be reformed in that institution.[4] In 1864 she published *Our Convicts*, in which the whole range of prison management in England was attacked and in which the Directorate of Convict Prisons was once more subjected to her scathing remarks.[5] Although she continued to manage Red Lodge Reformatory to the end of her life, Mary Carpenter found many other interests to occupy her once the reformatory schools had been safely established.

The founding of the Social Science Association in 1857 gave her a new medium for disseminating her ideas, which she did

---

[1] *Life and Work*, pp. 151–2.   [2] Ibid., p. 160.
[3] Qs. 970–972, p. 125. See also *Reformatory Schools*, pp. 314–315.
[4] *Transactions*, pp. 520–1.
[5] Jebb died in June 1863 and Mary Carpenter, who never mentioned his death, was very ill for the next two months (July/August 1863.) *Life and Work*, p. 235.

vigorously for twenty years.[1] In the same year, the indefatigable Mr. Adderley, M.P., carried an Industrial Schools Bill through the Commons and Mary Carpenter thus saw the realization of her second great plan.[2] She herself now arranged for the establishment of an industrial school in Bristol. Her interests became ever wider; convict discipline, workhouses, schools, the position of women in India and many other problems excited her interest and vigorous support. The Elementary School Act of 1876 realized the last of her great schemes. She remained active in all her undertakings until her death in June 1877.[3]

Red Lodge Reformatory

John Gittins has recently stated that the people who are likely to be attracted to approved school work would be extrovert and practical, perceptual rather than conceptual thinkers.[4] These characteristics are well illustrated in men like Turner, Jebb and Hall. Mary Carpenter, on the other hand, was strongly introvert and a conceptual rather than a perceptual thinker. A brief review of the institution which she managed for twenty-three years throws a very interesting light on the importance of these characteristics. Few people have thought more deeply or expressed more forcibly and clearly the theoretical principles on which an institution for children should be run. Yet Mary Carpenter never succeeded in creating the kind of institution which she had advocated and recommended for so many years. Unlike Turner and Jebb, she began with principles so firmly fixed that nothing that staff or children did could shake her convictions or lead her to view her problems in a different light. Mary Carpenter was a superb teacher but she never understood the methods of residential communal life as well as she under-

---

[1] Excepting the years when she was in India, she attended every meeting, reading one or two papers each time.

[2] 20 & 21 Vic., c. 48.

[3] Biographical material on Mary Carpenter is based on J. Estlin Carpenter, *The Life and Work of Mary Carpenter*, London, 1881 (first published 1879), 2nd Ed. R. J. Saywell, *Mary Carpenter of Bristol*, Bristol, 1964. F. P. Cobbe, 'Personal Recollections of Mary Carpenter', *Modern Review*, April 1880, pp. 279–300.

[4] 'Delinquency as Culture', *Oxford Review*, February 1966.

stood the methods of exciting and stimulating the interest of children at an intellectual level. She expected from children that, instead of relying on their own homes and their own parents, they should develop 'new affections and feelings . . . which usually either fill the unsatisfied void . . . or obliterate what is evil in those already formed and grievously polluted'.[1] The most fundamental principle was that the 'will' of the child must be involved in its own reformation.[2] The school must inspire a family feeling so that a child could look back on a 'happy home', and the staff must always be actuated by feelings of friendship for the child.[3] Whilst boys should be allowed 'as much liberty . . . as is found consistent with prudence', girls 'must be prepared for the natural restraints of the home'.[4] Meals should be eaten in silence and every facet of the child's life carefully planned, controlled and supervised. Any manifestation of behaviour that did not fit into the preconceived pattern had to be rigorously suppressed.

Red Lodge was the first girls' reformatory to be certified in England. The premises were bought by Lady Noel Byron in 1854 and the school was certified in December of that year. Mary Carpenter was the Lady Superintendent from its certification until her death in 1877. While Mary Carpenter was alive the inspectors were most reluctant to criticize her management even when they were thoroughly dissatisfied, in fear, no doubt, of some form of retaliation by her formidable pen. Whenever an inspector had cause to comment on an unsatisfactory point he went out of his way to suggest a reason for it, exonerating Miss Carpenter herself at the same time.

The administration of Red Lodge was governed by the most stringent regulations. A girl to be admitted 'must not be above fourteen and not a penitentiary case'.[5] She described those about to be admitted as

girls who will usually be found to be entirely devoid of any good principles of action, accustomed to the uncontrolled exercise of their will, particularly addicted to deceit both in word and actions, of

---

[1] Mary Carpenter, *Suggestions on the Management of Reformatories and Certified Industrial Schools*, London, 1864, p. 6.
[2] Ibid., p. 7.   [3] Ibid., p. 8.   [4] Ibid., p. 9.
[5] Mary Carpenter, *Red Lodge Girls' Reformatory School, Bristol. Its History, Principles, and Working*, Bristol, Arrowsmith, 1875, p. 3.

fair but misdirected powers, of violent passions, extremely sensitive to imagined injury and equally sensible to kindness.[1]

Her methods of reformation were:

1 Vigorous and all-pervading religious instruction in which, however, sectarian teaching was strictly forbidden.
2 Schooling in reading, writing and arithmetic and geography.
3 Industrial training, consisting of washing, ironing, cooking and needlework.
4 Definite provisions for innocent play (with dolls, toys, etc.), 'the activity of love and amusement natural to childhood'.[2]

The girls were divided into 'school girls' who were employed at least two hours a day in household work, three hours every afternoon in needlework, and 'a portion of the day' in knitting. (That left some three to three-and-a-half hours for actual schooling.) The older girls were occupied chiefly in the laundry and with other domestic chores. One hour a day was set aside for 'active exercise' by the girls.[3]

On admission a girl was not permitted to associate with the other girls but was kept in separate confinement. She was allowed to mix freely with other girls only when it appeared 'that she can do so without injury'.[4]

Girls were reminded that they were sent to Red Lodge 'in order to enable them to be honest and industrious members of Society in this world and to prepare them for another and a better'. Ten rules of conduct were read to every girl when she came to Red Lodge.

Another set of rules was laid down for the staff and these suggest an element of distrust which might account for the constant staffing difficulties which were experienced in Red Lodge. These rules included one that staff

must never converse with the girls respecting their past history which is to be confided to the Superintendent only; and they must carefully avoid any expression or mode of treatment calculated to awaken resentful feelings in the girls or make them feel themselves members of a degraded class.

Another rule stated that 'no intoxicating liquors except for

[1] Mary Carpenter, *Red Lodge Girls' Reformatory School* . . . , p. 3.
[2] Ibid., p. 4.   [3] Ibid., pp. 5–6.   [4] Ibid., p. 6.

medicinal purposes are to be admitted into the house'.[1]

Although Mary Carpenter was the only leading figure in the reformatory school movement who did not anticipate any difficulty in the staffing of such institutions, she had more trouble than most in finding the right officers.[2] In his first report made three years after the establishment of Red Lodge, Turner stated that 'the discipline errs perhaps on the side of kindness and indulgence. Miss Carpenter has not been as successful as she wished in engaging really efficient assistants'.[3]

At a time when Red Lodge only admitted girls on first conviction and none who were over thirteen, there were serious difficulties. In 1857 the behaviour of the girls was so bad that the local magistrates held a Petty Session in the school. Even then, rowdy behaviour continued. Mary Carpenter explained this by saying that 'there is a great want of moral force in the staff'.[4] Turner reported

gross misconduct of some very vicious girls who were in the first instance committed to prison for desertion and insubordination and afterwards discharged . . . a more efficient school mistress had been engaged and a stricter discipline enforced to the manifest advantage of the girls . . . comparing the school with other female reformatories I feel satisfied that the great desideratum in it is a really able matron.[5]

A cottage in the grounds of the school was set aside for older girls to prepare them for discharge and two senior girls went as domestic servants to Mary Carpenter's house but continued to sleep in the reformatory. When in 1860 Red Lodge published its first results, it was stated that, 'of the 33 girls discharged from the institution six had been discharged prematurely as incorrigible, 11 were doing well, 9 were doubtful and 7 had been

---

[1] Ibid., pp. 7–8. Mary Carpenter once said to Miss Cobbe: 'There never yet was man so clever but the matron of an institution could bamboozle him about every department of her business' (F. P. Cobbe, *Life of Frances Power Cobbe*, London, 1894, Vol. I, p. 306).

[2] *Select Comittee on Criminal and Destitute Juveniles*, 1852, Qs.1085–1095, pp. 137–138.

[3] *1st Report Reformatory Schools*, 1858, p. 24.

[4] R. J. Saywell, *Mary Carpenter of Bristol*, Bristol, Historical Assoc., 1964, p. 13.

[5] *2nd Report Reformatory Schools*, 1859, pp. 32–3.

re-convicted'.[1] 'It is an unwelcome fact', consoled Turner, 'that the percentage of reformation in the case of girls is uniformly found lower than in the case of boys.'[2] Turner's report for 1862 was rather more satisfactory: 'The manner of the girls appeared to be much more quiet and respectful and I was glad to find from the report and punishment books that there had been a decided improvement in general conduct.' This he put down to the fact that the majority of girls at Red Lodge were now very young and that several of the older and more troublesome inmates had been discharged. He also reported that Red Lodge was the cheapest girls' reformatory. (Annual cost per girl was £14 15s. od., compared with a national average of £18 16s. 5d.)[3]

In 1866 Mary Carpenter went to India and appointed a Miss Bailey to act as Lady Superintendent. At the same time, the matron resigned. Figures published for the period 1861 to 1864 showed that of 54 girls discharged, 33 were doing well, 8 had been re-convicted, and the fate of 13 was unknown. The inspector explained this by saying that the school was so well known that girls were sent to it from all over England. On discharge they scattered widely, which made it difficult to keep in touch with them.[4] A new matron was appointed to work under Miss Bailey, but she and the school teacher left within two years. In the absence of Mary Carpenter, the cost per girl per annum went up to £20 2s. 11d. (1869) and the inspector drew attention to the success rate of just over 60 per cent which put Red Lodge among the six least successful girls' reformatories in England. There was also further trouble.

The school had been very seriously disturbed by the insubordination of some of the girls towards the matron. The police were inadvisedly sent for and some of the ringleaders committed to prison. Responsibility for these unfortunate incidents did not rest with Miss Carpenter as she was then absent.[5] [Again, in the next year] . . . there had been a good many cases of misconduct . . . a spirit of disobedience and insubordination had crept in . . . [and again Turner commented

---

[1] *3rd Report Reformatory Schools*, 1860, p. 34.
[2] *4th Report Reformatory Schools*, 1861, p. 34.
[3] *6th Report Reformatory and Industrial Schools*, 1863, pp. 28–9.
[4] *9th Report Reformatory and Industrial Schools*, 1866, p. 33.
[5] *14th Report Reformatory and Industrial Schools*, 1871, pp. 10 and 51–2.

that] it is worthy to remark that Miss Carpenter with her long undoubted experience and knowledge of the subject acknowledges that the reformation of criminal girls is one of the most difficult and anxious tasks that anyone can take in hand.[1]

The matron and teacher were dismissed and new staff engaged, but still the conduct of the girls was unsatisfactory, and this was due.

to a change of officers, partly also to the inefficiency of some of them . . . I think the school has suffered in the last two or three years by the employment of a lady superintendent to whom Miss Carpenter had entrusted a great deal of the supervision of the institution . . . such intermediate authority gives interference without responsibility.[2]

The staff were changed again but the situation did not improve. In 1874 Turner complained of insufficient food, too much punishment and dullness of the girls.[3] There was a further change of matron in 1876; she only stayed for one year. In 1877 Mary Carpenter died. The inspector reported her death, made appropriate and sympathetic comments, and then proceeded to criticize the school in a manner very different from anything he had dared to do so far. 'I was totally dissatisfied not only with the education provided but also with the spirit and behaviour of the girls. . . . I find nothing in the condition of the school to give me satisfaction.'[4] In 1896 when Legge, the new Inspector, had made his first visit to Red Lodge, he wrote somewhat unkindly 'the school . . . still venerates the memory of Miss Mary Carpenter. There is, consequently, apt to be a tendency to rely too much on old methods and the fact is overlooked that methods which may have been suitable and even perhaps advisable forty years ago may be the very reverse now.'[5]

6 PRINCIPLES OF REFORMATION

The first Reformatory Schools Act of 1854[6] created a great deal of interest in the techniques and methods to be employed in

[1] *15th Report Reformatory and Industrial Schools*, 1872, p. 52.
[2] *16th Report Reformatory and Industrial Schools*, 1873, p. 50.
[3] *19th Report Reformatory and Industrial Schools*, 1876, p. 60.
[4] *21st Report Reformatory and Industrial Schools*, 1878, p. 55.
[5] *40th Report Reformatory and Industrial Schools*, 1897, p. 155.
[6] 17 and 18 Vic., c. 86.

establishing reformatories and a number of pioneers published guiding principles on how this might be done. The first of these was Barwick Lloyd Baker, the founder of the Hardwick Reformatory, who presented a paper on the subject at the British Association meeting in September 1854.[1] Baker rejected the new Agricultural School at Redhill as being too costly and reminded his listeners that the question of reformation of young offenders had to be treated in the general context of the management of crime. It was essential that elements of punishment must never be divorced from the practice of reformation: '. . . were punishments withdrawn from crime, not only the numbers of legal criminals would increase but . . . this very fact would increase the number of criminals at heart and give us a greater number to reform if we trusted to reformation solely. . . .'[2] He also warned against detaining boys too long in reformatories and made the interesting observation that whilst he thought he could effect a little reformation in a boy in one month, he doubted if he could hold out much hope for the future conduct of the boy who had been detained ten years.[3] A third principle was that a reformatory school should never offer advantages which were so superior to those available to the ordinary boy that they would incite envy. He realized that, given the social conditions of his day, this would be very difficult, but unless this principle was observed '. . . we should, I fear, have done a positive evil to the many which would outweigh whatever benefits we would give to the few'.[4] The only work that Baker regarded as appropriate was hard work on a farm. He did not think it necessary to teach boys any skills nor did he think that the education they were to be given should do more than stimulate a desire for further knowledge.[5]

The main influence on the boy was to be exercised by the managers of the school whose impact he visualized as being made mainly by the fact that they worked without reward other than the improved behaviour of the boys in their care. Although he employed a farm bailiff and a schoolmaster, he had no person in charge of the institution apart from himself and a

---

[1] Republished in *War with Crime* (being a Selection of Reprinted Papers on Crime, Reformatories, etc.), edited by H. Phillips and E. Verney, London, 1889, pp. 163–81.
[2] Ibid., p. 165.   [3] Ibid., p. 166.   [4] Ibid., p. 166.   [5] Ibid., p. 169.

fellow manager. Baker saw his main task, as, first, to calm the over-stimulated city boy: '. . . I know of no employment which will allay the excitement and tranquilize the mind, so as to prepare it to be acted upon by a firm kindness like steady hard digging.'[1] Secondly, by kindness and firmness to establish an influence over the boy and, thirdly, to prepare the boy for a simple life as an honest labourer. He did not see it as his function to stimulate and develop the more able lad: '. . . while on the one hand I would not attempt to repress them, I would not, on the other, allow their crime to be the direct cause of their elevation'.[2] Baker advised that reformatories be established in simple rough buildings. He objected strongly to the enormous structures which frequently housed institutions. His plan for the boys after training was to supervise them as long as possible by apprenticing them to farmers and asking 'neighbouring gentlemen' to report occasionally on the boy.

Three months later, Matthew Davenport Hill published his 'Practical Suggestions' in the form of a letter to Lord Brougham.[3] He first described the kind of child who would be admitted to a reformatory as being mainly wild, uncared for, living more or less by his wits, untaught, without occupation, restless and quick. He warned that one should not try to draw a comparison between ordinary children, whom he described as having 'head and heart duly nurtured' and therefore 'creatures of promise', with 'city arabs', whom he described as 'little stunted men' who must be turned into children again before they could be subjected to the right kind of influence. He also reminded his readers of the differential significance of wrong behaviour between these different groups of children: 'It is one thing to relapse into wrong in conformity with bad habits; quite another to strike into wrong in contradiction to good habits.'[4] Hill then turned his attention to the problem of staff and noted that only few teachers have the necessary sense of 'mission' to undertake this work. He strongly recommended the system employed at Mettray of engaging young teachers and selecting

[1] Ibid., p. 167. [2] Ibid., p. 170.
[3] *Practical Suggestions to the Founders of Reformatory Schools*, in a letter from the Recorder of Birmingham to Lord Brougham with his Lordship's answer. December 1854, 7 pages.
[4] Ibid., p. 3.

from them those who show a natural bent for residential work. On the question of the employment of the children in institutions, he also regarded it as more desirable to teach the children to work with 'zeal and industry', rather than teach them specific skills. He mentioned Mettray and the Rauhe Haus as having established agricultural work as the best form of employment, with additional nautical training or domestic service in view of the great shortage of good servants which, he said, existed at that time. He thought small units of about twenty boys would be best but pointed out that at this early stage there was, and should be, room for experiment. Finally, Hill strongly recommended that institutions should start with very small numbers because he regarded the tone of an institution as the most important single factor. The right tone could only be established if the staff could exercise 'an overwhelming influence' on the minds of their charges.

Hill's proposals were vague and superficial and the deliberate omission of any mention of Redhill stung Sydney Turner, who published a very much more solid set of suggestions three months later, this time in a letter addressed to C. B. Adderley, M.P., the originator of the 1854 Act.[1] Turner discussed first what he called the fundamental question of the size of the institution to be established and once again strongly advocated the 'family division'. He agreed that economically larger institutions were to be preferred, but he pointed out that in Redhill he had devised a system whereby one could combine the advantages of a large institution, with centralized catering facilities, with those of the small family-type cottage.

The type of boy likely to go into a reformatory would show 'singular precocity, deep-seated suspicion, the habitual forwardness of the young criminal, wild licence, independence, self-action, the excitements of appetite and passion, and the risks, suffering and pleasures that a young thief can usually look back on'.[2] What was needed, therefore, was personal study, personal association, individual care and influence. Kindly domestic discipline was required, aimed at building up in the boy self-control and self-regulation. To achieve this, his boys

[1] 'Reformatory Schools. A Letter to C. B. Adderley, Esq., M.P.', London, 1855, p. 31.
[2] Ibid., p. 4.

were able to earn a few pence a week for their work and with this money could purchase 'sundry little luxuries' such as coffee for breakfast, treacle with their pudding, sweets, fruit, postage stamps, knives, Sunday caps, etc. Misbehaviour was punished by fines which in turn meant the withdrawal of luxuries.[1] If this reward system failed, cells were used with a diet of bread and water for periods ranging from a few hours to a few days. The cell was unheated and should give the inmate 'just as much cold and privation and discomfort as proper regard to health, cleanliness and the making of a kindly impression on the offender will allow of'.[2] In a few cases where the use of the cells failed or was inappropriate, as, for example, in cases of indecency, cruelty or insolence and defiance of a master, he recommended the use of corporal punishment, provided that certain rules were adhered to. First, that it should only be administered by a common birch rod (the instrument normally used in schools); second, that it be inflicted with as much solemnity and formality as possible, 'the manner being of more consequence than the amount'; third, that the boy's companions be allowed, but not invited, to witness it; and, fourth, that the senior person in the institution (governor or superintendent) should administer the punishment himself.[3] The value of corporal punishment, Turner maintained, lay in the rareness with which it was used. He thought that 'as a general rule the number of punishment varies directly as the inefficiency of the master, i.e., as his inability or failure to command the respect and win the confidence of the boys'.[4]

Like Baker and Hill, Turner regarded agriculture as the best form of employment, but all employment within an institution should be based on a set of rules which were, firstly, that the work done by the boy should resemble as closely as possible the work done by an ordinary labourer; secondly, that the boy should never be under the impression that he was working for the profit of the school, but rather that he was working for himself; and, thirdly, that a boy was most likely to be successful in his work if he were assigned limited tasks which he could regard as his own and which would stimulate in the boy 'the instincts of exertion and mastery over difficulties'.[5] The education of boys

[1] Ibid., p. 10.   [2] Ibid., p. 11.   [3] Ibid., pp. 11–12.
[4] Ibid., footnote, p. 4.   [5] Ibid., p. 10.

need not be of a very high standard but the classroom, like the work situation, offered great opportunities for influencing a boy. 'I have seen many a hard, wilful lad brought to thoroughly like and obey his master through feeling that the latter had an interest in enlightening and informing him and took pains to do so.'[1]

Turner then turned his attention to the problem of staff and again set down a number of rules which could be used by those wishing to select staff for reformatory schools. He wanted, first, religious people, people who need not have outstanding talents but who should be men of 'earnestness, love and a sound mind'. Second, if they were trade instructors, they need not be superbly skilled, but should have sufficient command of their trade to be able to gain the scholars' confidence and respect. Thirdly, 'he must not have any physical defects or oddities of manner or appearance. A good countenance and manly figure are great helps to his influence'. The fourth rule was that a master should not be afraid or think too highly of himself to share in the boys' industrial training, to work with them and to get dirty with them. Finally, a master should not be engaged until he had some experience of the type of boy he would have to deal with.[2] In discussing likely recruits, Turner rejected the 'National' schoolmaster as being too closely oriented to academic achievement. He rejected the 'Ragged School' teacher as being unable to exercise discipline, but felt that the 'Union Schools' were most likely to provide the right kind of master. Perhaps with an eye on Hill, Turner wrote that 'it may be as well to observe that training by practice is the sort of preparation wanted, training by lectures and questions for reformatory work is emphatically moonshine; the man wants experience and 'till he has this he may know everything in theory, but he will be worth little practically'.[3] In a final comment on staff, Turner made the point that where a man has been engaged and has been found to be suitable, he should be paid sufficiently well to relieve him of any family or financial anxiety so that he can concentrate whole-heartedly on the task before him. He next considered the problem of after-care. Here again, Turner's practical experience

[1] 'Reformatory Schools. A Letter to C. B. Adderley, Esq., M.P.', London, 1855, p. 11.

[2] Ibid., pp. 17–19.   [3] Ibid., p. 21.

was very much to the fore and he suggested three possible alternatives. The first was to apprentice boys to masters with supervision not only of the boy but also of the master. A second and better alternative was for the transfer of a boy into the army. But the best form of disposal in Turner's opinion, was to send a boy to one of the colonies, 'to start him in a new country . . . that eventually separates him from all former associations. He has usually been much more a delinquent through circumstances than a criminal through choice.'[1] And Turner then stated his earnest conviction that most of the delinquency that reformatory schools had to deal with was due to the vice, filth and wretchedness that existed in some of the districts of the large towns. The question should not be why there were so many delinquents, but given the social situation in which so many children grew up, why there were not many, many more.

Turner's recommendations were practical and valuable and the clear grasp of the issues in institutional training which he demonstrated in this pamphlet was undoubtedly responsible for his appointment in 1857 as Inspector of reformatory schools.

[1] Ibid., p. 23.

Chapter 2

The System

The Act of 1854 authorized the establishment of reformatory schools. By 1858 there were over fifty schools, almost the highest number at any time in the nineteenth century.[1] Since offenders were now legally detained, the schools no longer made an effort to attract and persuade children to stay by the facilities and provisions they offered.[2] There was a good deal of theoretical material and practical experience to guide those who were setting up new institutions all over the country. Both English and Continental institutions had been described and frequently reported on and a whole series of Blue Books and private publications between 1835 and 1853 provided an extensive literature with the necessary information on which new institutions could be established. But other pressures and stresses determined the shape and form of institutions.

Once the voluntary principle had been accepted, it was open to any respectable person in the country to establish an institution. Most of the early managers disregarded the problem of staff and appear to have assumed that any calibre of staff under proper supervision would be sufficient.[3] Inevitably, therefore,

[1] The highest number of schools was fifty-four in 1877/1878. After that, numbers fell steadily until there were thirty-nine in 1900. The greater number in earlier years was probably due to the absence of industrial schools.

[2] Cf. *2nd Report Inspector Reformatory Schools*, 1859. 'There is [now] little of the petting and bribery which at the outset obtained here and there. The principle of duty is more clearly insisted on; persuasions less trusted to' (pp. 15–16).

[3] Cf. *1st Report Inspector Reformatory Schools*, 1858, speaks of the lack of efficient staff and notes that 'some have still to be retained who are but ill-suited to the work' (p. 8). At the *Conference of Managers of Reformatory and*

some institutions experienced a continuous series of staff changes and the difficulties associated with it, while others were more fortunate in appointing officers with a natural inclination for residential work who then assumed real control of the institution.[1] The inspectorate saw the importance of defining the respective roles of voluntary managers and paid staff clearly enough, but it was a long time before they felt sufficiently strong and influential to intervene with bad management on behalf of good staff.[2]

Even where the staff employed was of the right quality, they came without training, very often without experience and sometimes with rigid religious ideas. As a result, the discipline in the reformatories became very quickly more and more penal and restrictive, thus making a mockery of the bitter battle which

---

Industrial Schools (Edinburgh 1875), Mr. A. Falconer stated that 'the capital fault of our present state is the absence of a fixed rule as to the necessity for previous experience in all who superintend and govern'. *Record of Proceedings*, London, 1875, Reformatory and Refuge Union, p. 132.

[1] 4 boys' and 1 girls' reformatory had one superintendent for 20–30 years.

2 boys' and 1 girls' reformatory had one superintendent for 30–40 years.

2 boys' reformatories had one superintendent for 40 and 45 years respectively.

3 boys' reformatories had one superintendent for 18–26 years who in each case was succeeded by his son.

[2] Some idea of the early relationships between managers and superintendents can be obtained from their conference systems. There were two main organizations. The Reformatory and Refuge Union was founded by managers in 1856. It held its first three conferences in 1857, 1862 and 1866. These were attended by superintendents and matrons on grants provided by the Union. From 1869 onwards superintendents attended on more equal terms and the conferences, which were held triennially, published reports of conferences of managers, but it was not until 1899 that these reports were headed 'Conference of Managers and Superintendents'. These conferences continued until 1933 when the R. and R. Union became the Children's Aid Society. The National Association of Certified Reformatory and Industrial Schools was formed in 1881 to deal more specifically with certified schools because it was felt that the Union covered too wide a field. The Association held seven meetings, but merged with the Union in 1898. From 1899 the Union conference reports contain papers presented to the Association (see the various *Conference Reports*, and *50 Years' Record of Child Saving and Reformatory Works*, 1856–1906, being the Jubilee Report of the Reformatory and Refuge Union, London, 1906).

had been fought by some pioneers against the use of an exclusively restrictive policy in training children.[1]

The Victorian view that work was a virtue in itself, that habits of work had to be established in children, and that regularity of work habits was a necessary qualification for becoming a respectable citizen of the lower class, led to an excessive use of labour in many institutions. Since it was also considered to be a measure of an institution's worth to run it as cheaply as possible, and since it was necessary to convince those who subscribed funds towards the management of institutions that their money was being well spent, a number of undesirable factors became deeply entrenched. There was, first of all, a gradual trend from work carried out for training purposes to work which would increase profit. A number of institutions eventually confined themselves to industries which were not only useless in a training sense, but which were often very harmful to the children, in order to achieve a maximum profit from the labour force which the children represented. Amongst these destructive industries were brickmaking, wood chopping and paper salvage for boys, and laundrywork for girls.[2] Most of the institutions soon realized that the most valuable worker in terms of profitability was the older inmate, who had the training and experience to maintain a high level of production in the institution's industries. Not surprisingly, therefore, there was an almost universal tendency to retain the services of such inmates as long as possible. Reformation criteria of readiness for release on licence were largely ignored and many youngsters were detained for almost the full five years provided for in the Act, so that their period under licence was sometimes no more than a few weeks.[3] Nor was there much incentive to develop a licensing

[1] Some schools went so far as to introduce barred windows, locked doors and cropped hair. This went on well into the 1920s. See *First Report on the Work of the Children's Branch*, H.M.S.O., 1923, pp. 18–19.

[2] Cf. *22nd Report Inspector Reformatory and Industrial Schools*, 1879: 'The Managers have been requested to reduce the amount of labour applied to the brickfield' (p. 56).

[3] Cf. *15th Report Inspector Reformatory and Industrial Schools*, 1872: 'Unless a desire for improvement can be set up in the boy's heart by the influence of the school in a year or two, it is a waste of time, waste of money, waste of opportunity to retain him' (p. 77). *22nd Report Inspector Reformatory and Industrial Schools 1879*: 'I think the tendency to keep the boys to the end of their term of detention should be kept within reasonable limits' (p. 85).

system in a satisfactory way, and the frequent description of discharged children as 'doubtful' or 'not known' demonstrated the reluctance of institutions to maintain contact with discharged youngsters if this involved them in any great expenditure.[1] The corollary of excessive labour in institutions to minimize *per capita* expenditure was to provide a minimum of provisions and services and, in many institutions, buildings were hopelessly inadequate,[2] food insufficient in both quality and quantity,[3] and clothing quite inadequate to protect the children, particularly those who had to work the year round in exposed areas in every kind of weather.[4] Finally, the government's system of paying a *per capita* allowance for each child led many institutions to admit more children than they could properly cater for and to admit the wrong kind of child; that is to say, children who were really too young or too unsophisticated or too sick physically or mentally to be able to benefit from the institution programme.[5]

These various handicaps and difficulties determined not only

---

[1] Cf. *27th Report Inspector Reformatory and Industrial Schools*: 'When a large percentage of discharged children are returned [unknown], there must be something wrong in the management' (p. 14). In 1867 schools were offered an allowance for children on licence as an inducement to discharge them and the inspector spoke of limiting sentences of children of thirteen and over to three years. *11th Report Inspector Reformatory and Industrial Schools*, 1868, p. 5.

[2] Cf. *16th Report Inspector Reformatory and Industrial Schools*: 'The buildings . . . are not satisfactorily arranged . . . [there is] no bathroom or bathing place . . . closets are open to the playground' (182 boys), p. 46, or *20th Report*, 1877: 'The accommodation for the Superintendent . . . is totally inadequate. There is no provision for the sick. No attempt is made to place the school on an efficient footing' (p. 73).

[3] *5th Report Inspector Reformatory and Industrial Schools*, 1862. When two boys died in one school Turner put this down to incessant work and schooling and inadequate food (p. 33).

[4] *21st Report Inspector Reformatory and Industrial Schools*, 1878. Deaths in a school ship were ascribed by the inspector to insufficient and monotonous food, inadequate clothing and too much exposure in winter (pp. 58–59).

[5] Cf. *4th Report Inspector Reformatory and Industrial Schools*, 1861. Of every seven children admitted to Reformatories two were under twelve and four were first convictions (p. 9). Again, in the *22nd Report*, 1879, the inspector complained that too many children under twelve were admitted (p. 5). In 1880 (*23rd Report*, p. 8) the inspector warned school ships about accepting boys who were weak. Some of these faults were still in existence when Clarke Hall wrote in 1917. See *The State and the Child*, London, 1917, esp. pp. 67–70.

the structure and function of the reformatories but also the role the inspectorate came to play. It had been the intention of the pioneers that the voluntary reformatories should individually and independently develop their systems of reformation. In return for government certification and public funds, the schools would be open to an inspectorate which would evaluate and report on each institution to satisfy the public that the children committed by the courts were being reformed, but the problems which have been outlined forced the inspectorate into a role first and foremost of protecting the children and of trying to alleviate the worst hardships they were often subjected to.[1]

The motivating force of the pioneer institutions had been a concern with principles of reformation. Neither Jebb nor Turner nor Mary Carpenter assigned undue importance to financial and administrative problems. The schools which came to be established after the 1854 Act, however, were not managed in most cases by men who had given much thought to questions of principle and they were soon overwhelmed by problems of finance and, as has been shown, all the negative developments which governed the administration of reformatories were centred on financial considerations which to most represented a simple survival issue. Because it was a universal problem, the tendency was to find universal solutions and to rationalize these into principles. In this way, the schools, managed by men of widely differing temperament, knowledge and experience, nevertheless became a system rather than a network and, in spite of the voluntary principle, displayed more similarities than divergencies.

There were also two factors which led to ambivalent attitudes within the schools. These may be more readily comprehensible in the light of modern sociological theory. The first was concerned with the fear of offering the offender advantages which

[1] This applied throughout the nineteenth century, as can be seen from the following quotation: 'Since Truant Schools first came into existence, I have never ceased to protest against the strict treatment, the excess of corporal punishment, and the absence of recreation or anything like reward for good conduct.' The inspector spoke of schools 'into which I have never entered without feeling more sympathy for the inmates than for the Truant School system' (*38th Report Inspector Reformatory and Industrial Schools*, 1895, p. 32).

were denied to his honest counterpart and the second was concerned with the question of preliminary imprisonment.

The movement for the establishment of voluntary reformatory schools was at its strongest some twenty years before the establishment of universal compulsory education in England and at a time when the children of very large sections of the population lived in states of extreme poverty and social deprivation. It was not surprising that a constantly recurring criticism of the provisions for young delinquents was based on the argument that it was only by committing a crime that a child could gain access to education and industrial training. Lord Chief Justice Denman expressed a widely felt attitude when he said, 'I am myself extremely jealous of the gratuitous instruction of the young felon in a trade, merely because he is a felon'.[1] Mary Carpenter dealt with this problem by arguing that all the poor sections of society had access to cheap schools and that reformatories, by taking the more awkward children, made the job of the schools that much easier.[2] Martineau also devoted a great deal of space to a discussion of this problem but rejected the view that the young delinquent was being offered an advantage because, she argued, since the young offender dreaded committal to a reformatory and certainly did not regard it as an advantage, it should be seen from his point of view.[3] The managers of the reformatories were always acutely conscious of this difficulty and endeavoured to find a solution by providing what they did provide in a manner unlikely to attract and be pleasant to the young offender. Thus, the education provided was poor in quality,[4] the work was hard, the bulk of what the children earned was retained by the institution, and the buildings, food and clothing left much to be desired. Some managers took this attitude even further by denying the right of any former inmate of a reformatory to achieve a 'specially good appointment in the world'.[5] The application of Merton's

[1] Quoted by Jebb: *Report on the Discipline and Management of the Convict Prisons*, London, 1851, p. 103.

[2] *Reformatory Schools*, pp. 40–1.   [3] *Edinburgh Review*, op. cit., pp. 402–15.

[4] Cf. *10th Report Inspector Reformatory and Industrial Schools*, 1867. 'The business of a Reformatory is to correct rather than instruct' (p. 8), and *20th Report*, 1877: 'The educational standard aimed at is not a high one' (p. 4).

[5] L. G. Baker, *Report of 5th Conference National Association Reformatory and Industrial Schools*, Birmingham, 1891, p. 125.

theory of anomie might explain the unexpected success of reformatories, which in spite of the very meagre provisions they offered, nevertheless managed to achieve a success rate[1] of about 75 per cent for their inmates throughout the nineteenth century. Using this theory, we could say that the majority of children committed to reformatory schools were, by definition, in a state of anomie. The schools offered them, usually for the first time, some access to institutional means for achieving cultural goals.[2] However, once compulsory education had been established and all children of the lower classes had been afforded similar access to institutional means there had to be a pronounced and continuous process of change for the better in the material, educational and industrial facilities offered by the reformatories, if they were to continue with the same good results. And there was.

The founders of the movement for reformatory schools were pioneers in the sense that they were responsible for the formulation and introduction of social change, but once compulsory education had been introduced, the ideas which were once revolutionary tended to become reactionary, and from the mid-1870s onwards the founders of the reformatory schools and many who followed in their wake, were overtaken by social forces they could not accept. The central issue in which the managers became involved was the question of whether or not a convicted juvenile offender should undergo a short period of imprisonment before entering a reformatory. Three reasons were usually offered as justification for this spell in prison. One was a simple administrative one. It took time after committal to find a school and ascertain if the managers were willing to take a given child. During this time the child had to be detained somewhere and prison was an obvious choice. A second reason was that a reformatory was concerned only with reforming offenders. Since a crime had been committed, there should also be punishment. If it was not the business of a reformatory to punish, then this must be carried out prior to admission, i.e., in

---

[1] Children not re-convicted within three years of their discharge from a reformatory.

[2] R. K. Merton, *Social Theory and Social Structure*, New York, 1957, especially Chapter IV, 'Social Structure and Anomie'.

prison.[1] Thirdly, it was argued that a young offender, following his committal, would be in a state of 'high excitement' which was not conducive for the commencement of reformation. It was argued that a calming period in prison would create the proper frame of mind in the youngster and make him receptive to what the reformatory had to offer.

Those who were opposed to previous imprisonment put forward four counter-arguments. They said that the practice deprived prison of its terrors, that it corrupted children by bringing them into contact with older criminals, that it cast a permanent taint on their characters and added to a youngster's difficulties when he resumed life in the community.[2]

By the 1880s the judiciary,[3] the inspectorate,[4] the managers of Scottish schools[5] and public opinion were firmly opposed to the continuation of the practice. Only the English managers held out with surprising obstinacy. Perhaps it would be justified to explain the position of the managers in the light of recent work on 'inmate sub-cultures'.[6] A committal to a reformatory was a very long sentence. This, coupled with the consequent separation from parents, must have produced an extreme state of anxiety which the Victorians described as 'high excitement'. In this state the youngster could be expected to be extremely rebellious and highly susceptible to the influence of other youngsters, or, in contemporary language, to the impact of the inmate sub-culture. By placing the child in solitary confinement immediately after committal, the managers intuitively resolved this situation, because they could expect the extreme anxiety to be followed by a state of depression and apathy,

---

[1] *The Royal Commission* of 1884, which wanted to abolish previous imprisonment, suggested alternative punishments, thus upholding this principle, see para. 37. This issue is still not entirely resolved. A recent paper suggested that 'punishment and treatment need to be provided for quite separately' (see H. Arden, 'Integration of Approved Schools with the Child Care Service'. *Conference of Association of Municipal Corporations and County Councils Association*, 1966, p. 50).

[2] *Royal Commission*, 1884, para. 37.

[3] *Report to the Secretary of State, Home Dept., on the state of the law relating to the Treatment and Punishment of Juvenile Offenders*, 1881.

[4] *36th Report Reformatory and Industrial Schools*, 1892, p. 16.

[5] *34th Report Reformatory and Industrial Schools*, 1890, p. 11.

[6] See especially D. Clemmer, *The Prison Community*, New York, 1958 (1941); and G. M. Sykes, *The Society of Captives*, Princeton, 1958.

which made the newcomer easier to handle. They could also expect the child in this acute phase of deprivation to be more susceptible to kind adults and less susceptible, once the adults had staked their claim on him, to the more negative aspects of the influence exerted by other inmates.[1]

Whatever the moral justification for such an attitude may be, it would certainly have made the opposition of English managers meaningful, if it is assumed that their primary interest was the smooth running of their institutions. Without some explanation, the views of managers and their stubborn refusal to follow Parliament and people are incomprehensible, especially after an Act of Parliament (1893) made previous imprisonment optional.[2]

The question of previous imprisonment was the most important issue in the alienation of public feeling towards reformatories, but it was not the only one.[3] During the 1870s the incidence of juvenile delinquency seemed to be falling[4] and some of the most ardent supporters of reformatory schools took the view that since these schools had done the job they had set out to do, that is to say, reforming those youngsters who were criminal and deterring those who were about to become so, they should now give way to more enlightened provisions.[5]

---

[1] See Memorandum A, *Departmental Committee on Reformatory and Industrial Schools* 1896, p. 156: '. . . boys are more apt to be influenced by other boys than by their master, unless the master happens to be a remarkable man or is thrown with them into close intimacy.' The way in which relationships were developed in this situation is well described by Charles Reade, *It's Never Too Late to Mend*, London, 1896 (1857).

[2] See the *Report of the Council of the Nat. Assoc. of Certified Reformatory and Industrial Schools* 1894: 'The Council cannot refrain from remarking that [Lord Leigh's Act of 1893] was very undesirable . . . there are some schools where previous imprisonment will still be insisted on', pp. 16–17.

[3] *The Council Report of the National Assoc. of Certified Reformatory and Industrial Schools* 1891 (p. 2) contains these words: 'There exists in the public mind a great deal of uncertainty as to the value of the Reformatory and Industrial School system and unsound views on questions affecting them largely obtain.' In 1894 the President of the Nat. Assoc. complained that: 'Attacks are constantly being made upon the schools and the value of their work openly questioned' pp. 2–3.

[4] *Reformatory and Industrial Schools Commission* 1884, para. 3.

[5] Thus, Lord Norton who, as Charles Adderley, had been largely responsible for the 1854 Act, was campaigning in 1881 for the abolition of reforma-

Many reformatories, as we have seen, were either very rough or very inadequate. With every year that passed their condition deteriorated, the demands made on them increased, but the means of improving them were lacking.[1] Public funds were only provided for the actual maintenance of inmates, and voluntary subscriptions for buildings and improvements decreased steadily until towards the end of the century they represented a minute fraction of the over-all cost of the schools.[2] As Turner pointed out as far back as 1855, the more centralized and rigid an institution and the larger the number of inmates, the cheaper it would be to run. This factor had led to the establishment of the great institutional systems which were so characteristic of the period but, here again, the more it became recognized that the neat, orderly, rigidly controlled institutions were destructive in their effect on the growth and development of young children, the greater the revulsion became.[3] Since it was the small reformatories which tended to be the more successful and small reformatories were usually run by a superintendent and his wife, there was a consequent shift of emphasis in the reformatory school system from the managers to the superintendents. Yet another consequence of the general trend towards making provisions for all children was that the reformatory school child

---

tory and industrial schools and their replacement by 'Schools for neglected and destitute children'. *Report Conference of Managers*, 1881, p. 34.

[1] Cf. *38th Report Inspector Reformatory and Industrial Schools*, 1895: 'Buildings which 20 years ago would have received a certificate without remonstrance would not be considered satisfactory now' (p. 10). See also Memorandum A. *Departmental Committee on Reformatory and Industrial Schools*, p. 156, '[Lack of funds] has been the cause of grievous defects in these schools'.

[2] In 1860 the total cost of reformatories was £92,854 5s. 6d. of which £24,903 6s. 7d. was contributed by voluntary subscriptions. In 1880 total cost was £134,079 16s. 8d. of which £5,005 0s. 4d. was voluntarily subscribed. See *24th Report Inspector Reformatory and Industrial Schools*. The Conference of Managers 1881 was told by Lord Norton that in 1880 public funds provided 90 per cent of the cost of schools, private subscriptions 7 per cent, and parents of inmates 3 per cent. See *Report*, p. 55.

[3] The Conference of Managers of Reformatory and Industrial Institutions 1884 heard two papers on the dangers of institutional life. See *Report*, pp. 26–30; 'The Care of Pauper Children', and pp. 53–7, 'Independent Inspections for Uncertified Schools and Homes'. Already in 1878 a local government report, *The Home and Cottage System of Training and Educating the Children of the Poor*, strongly urged the adoption of small cottages with the 'family system' for children's institutions, pp. 8–9.

who, even in a poorly equipped school, had enjoyed advantages which were denied to many children outside such institutions, was now becoming increasingly handicapped when he left his school after prolonged industrial training. He could not compete on equal terms with those children who had the advantage of elementary schooling.

The government hoped and expected that its inspector, Colonel Inglis, would, by his influence on the managers, induce them to improve the condition of the schools, but Inglis was weak, the managers were strongly defensive, and there were frequent clashes of will in which the managers refused to give way.[1] As a next step, a Royal Commission was set up in 1883 'to enquire and report upon the operation, management, control, inspection, financial arrangements and condition generally of certified Reformatories . . . in order to run such institutions more efficiently for the object with which they were established'. The report of this Commission, which was published in 1884, is surprisingly weak. The Commissioners seemed to have had no taste for a systematic examination of the problems involved and were unwilling to commit themselves in any way towards a system of child management. In this respect their report stands in marked contrast to that of the Commission which sat and reported twelve years later.

Most of the weaknesses in the reformatory school system which have already been described were mentioned by the Commissioners and they made a series of recommendations all of which were designed to repair and maintain the existing system rather than calling for any fundamental changes. Even so, quite a number of these recommendations were strongly attacked by the managers as representing a gross interference in what were supposed to be independent schools.[2] As far as the management of the schools was concerned, the Commission reiterated the value of the voluntary principle without, however,

---

[1] The example of the Truant Schools has already been cited. Inglis ordered the schools to display lists of punishments awarded, but most schools refused to do this. See *Commission 1884*, para. 39.

[2] The Conference of Managers which followed the publication of the Commission Report passed two resolutions attacking the educational recommendations and the recommendations concerning discharges from reformatories. See *Report* 1884, pp. 80 and 95.

examining its real implications. They also reminded the inspector of his right to withdraw the certificate from sub-standard schools and instructed him to keep a close watch on the qualifications and efficiency of superintendents. They urged the selection of women managers, especially for girls' schools, and schools for younger children, and expressed a view that reformatories should either be small or, if large, should be sub-divided into small units. They urged that all non-educational industries should be abolished, the profit motive in children's work should be eliminated, education should be given more importance and should be improved, and the schools should be inspected more frequently. They thought that when children under fourteen or on first conviction were sent to a reformatory, a special report should be submitted by the committing magis-trates stating their reason for such a step and the children should only be committed up to the age of sixteen or for a period of from three to five years. Managers were to state in writing their reasons for refusing admission to any child. They debated the issue of previous imprisonment; the Commissioners decided against it and suggested that boys should be whipped instead prior to admission to a reformatory and girls should be subjected to a period of solitary confinement, but not in a prison. The Commissioners made six recommendations designed to restrict the use of punishment in reformatories and advocated the establishment of special reformatories for 'refractory cases' with a proviso that children sent to such special institutions must be paid for by the reformatory transferring them, so as not to swamp those new institutions with all the children who might present any form of difficult behaviour. As might be expected, the Commissioners asked for greater use to be made of licens-ing, with a special report from the inspector where this was not being done. They wanted to see more halfway hostels for children discharged on licence and they wanted more care and accuracy in the returns submitted by the managers on the dis-posal and successes of the inmates.

The Royal Commission of 1884 did not question the need for the kind of schools they were dealing with. They made it their concern to examine the ways in which the schools operated, and based their recommendations on factors which were essen-tial but which were not carried out as efficiently and as effectively as they should be. The 1896 Committee[1] on the other hand tackled their job very much more thoroughly and at considerably greater depth. They presented an enormous report which in many ways is among the best publications on institutional practice and management, and they not only concerned themselves with the things that were being done and the way they were being done but more important with the principles underlying the things that were done. They had the courage to examine the rightness or wrongness of these principles and to comment on them. The result of this approach had three main consequences. First it led to the fairly widespread rejection of the report by the schools and more particularly by managers.[2] Secondly, it caused a great deal of disunity amongst the members of the Committee itself leading them to submit no less than nine memoranda with their main report.[3] Thirdly, it gave voice to a fundamental conflict in the management of young offenders. This conflict revolved around two questions. The first of these concerned the problem of the criteria to be used to decide whether or not a child should be placed in residential care. The Committee felt that no child should be removed from home unless the conditions of that home and the situation of the child were such that no other alternative would have been satisfactory. This they regarded as no more than basic justice not only to the child that was being deprived of its home life but also to the community which had to pay to maintain the child in the institution. But they also acknowledged the existence of what they described as the 'asylum' theory which held that a decision of whether or not to place a child in an institution should always be based on whether or not this was ultimately in the best interest of the child, in other words whether it would offer the child the best and most desirable

---

[1] *Report of the Departmental Committee on Reformatory and Industrial Schools* C, 8204, H.M.S.O., 1896.

[2] The National Association of Reformatory and Industrial Schools drew up a memorandum citing fifteen major objections to the report. They presented a strongly worded protest to the Secretary of State on 19 March 1897, in which they accused many Committee Members of being hostile, biased and ignorant. See *Report of the Council of the Association to the Conference* of 1897, pp. 28–38.

[3] *Report of the Departmental Committee*, 1896, pp. 155–74.

opportunities for its ultimate progress.[1] The second issue in the conflict was concerned with young offenders specifically. Having once decided that a child should be placed in an institution the question arises that if the child is an offender would it be best to help such a child by placing it in a situation where it must mix with other offenders, many of whom are likely to be worse in their criminal sophistication than the child itself, or would it be better to seek alternative methods of dealing with young offenders by putting them into environments in which the right moral attitudes prevail unhindered by harmful influences?[2]

These questions are fundamental not only to the period under discussion but require to be answered by every generation that has to deal with young offenders. The other outstanding feature of the 1896 Report was the importance it attached to the child itself. The previous commission took the view that reformatory and industrial schools were essential to control young offenders to protect the community. While they recognized that the offender had a right to be fairly and properly treated in the institution, they nevertheless regarded the institutions as being more important in relation to society than the child itself. The 1896 Committee on the other hand regarded the child and its welfare as the most important single factor in the operation of these schools. Although they fully subscribed to the class differences between children in these schools and their mentors[3] and although they had no hesitation in expressing their full support of this class division they nevertheless viewed the schools as primarily instruments for offering children a happy and constructive environment.[4] Implicit in this approach was an assumption that the kind of children who would find their way into these schools were not bad but wrong, that they did not need punishment so much as correction and help. To help them was not charity but an essential and humane task from which the community could be expected to gain as much as the children themselves. It is important to stress this point because it was the Committee of 1896 which clearly and explicitly rejected the very foundations on which the great pioneers of the reformatory school movement had established

[1] Ibid., p. 84.   [2] Ibid., p. 84. See also Memorandum A, pp. 155–8.
[3] Ibid., p. 20.   [4] Ibid., p. 102.

their schools.[1] Much of the confusion in aims and objectives that has been a feature of the schools' history for so many years is based on this factor. Following the 1896 Committee Report the public would ask whether the schools were run in the interests and for the well-being of the children, while many of the managers and heads of schools would continue to operate as though Mary Carpenter and Berwick Lloyd Baker were still the proper guides for their responsible tasks.

This confusion about school functions was further increased by the decision of the Departmental Committee to treat reformatory and industrial schools as one because 'there is no substantial difference in the discipline and regime beyond what can be accounted for by difference of age'.[2] The inspectorate tended to agree with this view and while the Committee's observations were undoubtedly correct they were nevertheless based on yet another confusion of principle. Reformatory schools had been established to deal with young offenders at a time when no general provisions existed for children in need. Industrial schools were subsequently added to absorb the larger but criminally less important sections of the neglected child population. This was done partly as a measure to prevent juvenile crime and partly as a humanitarian (i.e. religious) duty to fill the gap between offenders catered for in prisons and reformatories and destitute children catered for by charitable organizations which had their major growths also in this period.[3] Industrial schools were intended for what Mary Carpenter called children of the 'perishing classes'.[4] What the Departmental Committee failed to note was that the similarity between reformatory and industrial school children was no

---

[1] The Memorandum to the Secretary of State (q.v.) claimed that by ignoring the moral and religious significance of the schools the report failed to 'grasp the true proportions of the subject'. See *Report to the Conference*, 1897, p. 37.

[2] *Report of the Departmental Committee*, 1896, p. 45.

[3] Industrial schools were established in 1857, the Muller homes were started in 1854, Barnardo started in 1866 and Stephenson (National Children's homes) in 1869.

[4] 'Those who have not yet fallen into actual crime but who are almost certain from their ignorance, destitution and the circumstances in which they are growing up, to do so if a helping hand be not extended to them.' See *Reformatory Schools*, London, 1851, p. 2.

greater than the similarity between children in industrial schools and in children's homes.

By the end of the century the trend of development was thus the opposite of what the prototypal institutions had found to be effective. Whereas they introduced a division of intake and management for their populations, the school system moved towards unification. With the abolition of imprisonment before admission to a reformatory,[1] the external differentiation between the two types of schools disappeared.[2]

2 STABILIZATION OF THE SYSTEM

The events and changes of the last quarter of the nineteenth century created a system which had made good progress in such areas as health[3] and vocational training,[4] but its basic functions had been undermined and its financial arrangements were totally inadequate.[5] The managers, already in conflict with public opinion over the question of imprisonment, were disillusioned about the committee of 1896 and many lost interest in the schools. The superintendents lived in considerable isolation from each other and from the community[6] and wielded increasingly greater power within the schools. Local authorities had been involved in the work of the schools since 1870 but only

[1] Reformatory Schools Act 1899, 62 & 63 Vic. c. 12.

[2] It is noteworthy that the most recent plans once again envisage a differentiation (by age and criminality) between approved schools and more punitive treatment systems for young offenders.

[3] Thus whilst the *Final Report of the Anthropometric Committee* (by C. Roberts and R. W. Rawson, London, 1882–1883) reported industrial school boys of fourteen to be shorter and lighter in weight than comparable children in day schools, Legge reported in 1899 that schools had to introduce inter-school sports because their superiority in competitions with elementary schools was such that day schools refused to compete. *43rd Report*, 1899, p. 41.

[4] The interest in vocational training is well illustrated in a series of papers to the Triennial Conference in 1905, see *Conference Report Reformatory and Refuge Union*, 1905, esp. pp. 7–30.

[5] An Inter-departmental committee (Home Office – Treasury and Board of Education) failed to solve this. See *Interdepartmental Committee on the Provision of Funds for Reformatory and Industrial Schools*, 1906 (2 vols.).

[6] *Certified Schools Gazette*, 13:3, 1920, p. 25.

in industrial schools through their education committees.[1] Because managers were rarely heard some of the superintendents now began to assume leadership of the system and to act as spokesmen for it. Among the most notable perhaps were C. Oxley who fought so ably for superannuation and pension schemes for school staff; J. D. Johnson who tried to introduce new educational methods into the schools; Brother Finn Barr[2] who wanted to improve after-care methods; and Israel Ellis, the dynamic spokesman for the schools for nearly thirty years. In 1905 the superintendents established a Social Union which arranged for an annual dinner at which prestigious members of the Home Office were to speak each year.[3] In 1908 the famous Children's Act was passed,[4] which showed that magistrates had no less than twelve alternatives for dealing with young offenders. It provided for grants to the schools from local authorities and these two factors contributed to a fall in committals, partly because there was so much choice and partly because local authorities were reluctant to pay and exerted pressure to reduce admissions.[5] It was probably in 1908 that the Society of Superintendents was formed and produced the *Certified Schools Gazette*, the forerunner of the *Approved Schools Gazette*.[6]

The whole trend of the 'Children's Charter', as the Act of 1908 is often called, was aimed at a more comprehensive and child-orientated legal system, and at more generous and liberal

[1] Thus in 1911 none of the 37 reformatories were run by Local Authorities, but 22 of 112 industrial schools were. See *Departmental Committee Report*, 1913, pp. 5–6.

[2] Only the life of Brother Finn Barr has been recorded. See C. M. Cluderay, *To Brighter Worlds*, Life of Brother Finn Barr, Dublin, 1958.

[3] *Seeking and Saving*, vol. xv, 1905, pp. 571 and 633.

[4] 8 Edw. VII, c. 67.

[5] See presidential address, First Conference of the Society of Superintendents, *Seeking and Saving*, vol. xvii, 1910, pp. 298–299. The chief inspector thought that more children would be admitted – ibid., p. 61 – but admitted in his *Report for 1909* (53rd) that committals had fallen.

[6] The *Certified Schools Gazette* was published as 'The Organ of the Society of Superintendents' as a monthly journal and probably issued its first number in September 1908. As far as I have been able to ascertain, there is no complete set of the *Gazette* in existence. My information is based on seventy-two odd numbers kindly lent to me by Mr. H. Cohen of Finnart House. They range from 1909–1926 and represent about a third of the actual issues (228). The *Gazette* changed its name in 1933.

provisions for children in all walks of life. The Act differentiated between reformatory and industrial schools by providing for local education authority payments for children in industrial schools, at the same time widening the scope of their intake to cover all classes of 'deprived' children, whilst reformatories were to receive payments from municipal and county councils. But the Act also brought the schools together by making transfers between them possible, thus following the trend set by the Committee of 1896. But since the 1896 Committee also challenged the ideas of the universal value of residential care for deprived and delinquent children and the difficulties of rehabilitating delinquents in delinquent environments, the logical next step should have been the separation of reformatory and industrial schools, reserving the former for the remedial treatment of young offenders along the lines of the new Borstal system, whilst the latter should have been merged into the educational system as State boarding schools.[1]

The Akbar affair

Before the system had any real opportunity to absorb and adjust to the many changes that had taken place, it was subjected to a severe test, for which it was so ill-prepared that the reactions to it created a pattern from which the schools have not been able to escape.

On 22 October 1910 *John Bull* carried a fearful story of 'Reformatory School Horrors – How boys at the Akbar School are Tortured – Several Deaths'. The account was based on information sent to the paper by Mr. and Mrs. Adams, ex-deputy superintendent and matron at the Akbar (Heswall) Nautical Training School. There were seven charges which included accusations that boys were gagged before being birched, that sick boys were caned as malingerers, that boys

[1] At the turn of the century the children in these schools were openly described as different (cf. Memorandum to Secretary of State from the Council of the National Association of Reformatories and Industrial Schools, 1897, *Conference Report*, p. 36). It would seem that this view is still implicitly accepted today when it is considered that the proposed changes which will finally separate young offenders from socially deprived children envisages placing the deprived into a child-care rather than an educational system.

were drenched with cold water as a punishment and were kept
standing all night for trivial offences[1] and most serious of all,
that boys had died as a result of punishments. Adams first
reported his charges to the Home Office. Chief Inspector T. D.
Robertson, a comparatively weak and ineffectual person,
investigated and rejected the charges. Following the publication
of this story the Home Secretary (Winston Churchill) appointed
C. F. G. Masterman, then Under-Secretary of State, Home
Office,[2] to lead an enquiry but Capt. Beuttler and others concerned in the charges were not suspended from duty.[3]

Even before Masterman reported, the Home Office adopted
an attitude that was, at best, suspicious. They refused to allow
John Bull to brief counsel on behalf of witnesses. They did not
intervene when two boys, due to give evidence at the enquiry,
absconded and subsequently pleaded with a Liverpool magistrate to send them to prison for protection.[4] A month later it
was reported that one of these boys had given his evidence and
as a result of frequent birchings had attempted to cut his throat.[5]
Masterman presented his report in March 1911[6] in which he
rejected all charges of brutality but confirmed that irregular
punishments had taken place. *John Bull* was highly incensed. It
accused the government of 'White-Washing'[7] and reiterated all
the charges. It quoted a scathing comment from *Nation* which
argued that if 'the Home Office concludes that the case for the
dismissal of the superintendent responsible . . . fails on the
ground that he had greatly ameliorated the boys' condition,
what kind of hell on earth must this institution once have been?'
John Bull persisted with its attacks and accused those involved

[1] B. Meilen who has recorded his experiences in a naval approved school
in the 1940s (*The Division*, London, 1967) in novel form described the same
punishments vividly. I. G. Briggs (*Reformatory Reform*, London, 1924) who
was in a reformatory about the time of the Akbar affair also described
severe irregular beatings (pp. 52–4).

[2] It is difficult to understand why Churchill should have chosen someone
both politically and (through his position in the Home Office) personally
involved.

[3] *John Bull*, 24 December 1910.

[4] Ibid., 7 January 1911.

[5] Ibid., 11 February 1911.

[6] *Report of Inquiry by C. F. G. Masterman, M.P., into charges made concerning
the management of the Heswall Nautical School*, Cd. 5541, H.M.S.O., 1911.

[7] *John Bull*, 4 March 1911.

of playing party politics over this.[1] In April it lead with a head-
line, 'Grave Home Office Scandal', in which it was claimed
that Chief Inspector Robertson had gone to the school and
threatened members of the staff who had given evidence against
Beuttler with dismissal for disloyalty[2] and that 'loyal' members
of staff were given an extra month's salary.[3] The Home Office
remained silent and on 14 May some 7,000 people took part in
a public protest meeting over the affair. The steward of the
school, who had also given information to *John Bull*, was discharged for misappropriating stores but the charge was dismissed by the magistrates.[4] Both Masterman and *John Bull*
exploited the Akbar affair to the full during the elections, when
Masterman was a candidate for Bethnal Green.[5] Labour
Members of Parliament had voted with the Government over
the question of Beuttler's dismissal but by October of that year
George Lansbury publicly regretted that decision. In a letter to
Mr. Adams he wrote: 'There is no excuse. We all voted wrong'.[6]
Within the schools the Report and Capt. Beuttler were supported without hesitation. It was felt that the Report was
fair and thorough, that the hostile witnesses had been fully
discredited and that 'Mr. Beuttler must elicit the sympathy of
everyone who understands what it all means'.[7] As a direct
result of the Akbar affair, however, Mr. Churchill appointed a
Departmental Committee with very wide terms of reference to
enquire into the constitution, management, discipline and
education of reformatory and industrial schools in England and
Wales. C. F. G. Masterman who had recommended such a
committee in his report was appointed chairman.[8]

[1] Ibid., 18 March 1911.　　[2] Ibid., 8 April 1911.

[3] Ibid., 15 April 1911. See also *Hansard, Fifth Series*, vol. xxiii, 1911 Cols.
1151 and 2008.

[4] *John Bull*, 27 May 1911.　　[5] Ibid., 29 July 1911.

[6] Ibid., 14 October 1911.

[7] *Seeking and Saving*, vol. xvii, 1911, pp. 447–8. In spite of the general
upheaval, Beuttler was felt to be so completely vindicated that the triennial
Conference of the Reformatory and Refuge Union in June 1911 made no
reference to the affair and Beuttler presented a paper on 'Nautical training
for Boys'. See *Conference Report*, 1911, esp. pp. 109–12. However, one
member of the Conference thought that the effects of the affair were
'keenly felt'. See H. Newman, 'Present Position of Reformatory and
Industrial Schools', *Friends' Quarterly Review*, October 1911.

[8] *Seeking and Saving*, op. cit., pp. 459–60.

The Akbar affair tested the divergence of view put forward in the Departmental Committee Report of 1896. It was a case of which comes first, the schools or the children. Following this incident the public argued for children first, whilst the schools opted for the protection of the system.[1]

Before the effects of the Akbar affair had subsided, the *Daily Mail* carried six articles under the heading 'Schools for Crime'[2] in which reformatories were strongly attacked because they did not classify their intake; were not staffed by men trained in 'prison routine'; boys lacked proper supervision; and for being under voluntary instead of state control. The schools responded, significantly, by rejecting a more prison-like pattern as being out of date and by emphasizing their severe discipline with some pride. Thus one school criticized in the articles claimed to give home leave only after three years' good conduct and that parents were only permitted to visit once in three months.[3]

There can be no doubt that the political leaders in the Home Office were greatly embarrassed over the question of certified schools. Chief Inspector Robertson was removed in October 1911[4] and because the inspectorate came under the terms of reference of the new Committee an acting chief inspector took over for the following eighteen months.

The Departmental Committee of 1913[5]

As a result of the recent upheavals the Committee, more than any other dealing with the schools, concerned itself with problems of the administration, control and public image of certified

[1] Note the similarity between these divergent responses in this affair and in the Court Lees affair of 1967.

[2] *Daily Mail*, 4–11 September 1911, by E. Bowen Rowlands.

[3] *Seeking and Saving*, vol. xvii, 1911, pp. 556–8, and *Certified Schools Gazette*, vol. 4, 1911, pp. 19–22. This outspokenness seemed to be typical. The *Daily Chronicle* (17 May 1916) carried an article on Juvenile Crime by C. McEnay in which he charged that 'no one with the faintest respect for childhood can regard the average reformatory as anything but an institution for blighting the lives of those who enter it'.

[4] See *Seeking and Saving*, vol. xvii, 1911, p. 573. Robertson was 'promoted' Commissioner for Prisons in Scotland. He died in February 1913.

[5] *Report of the Departmental Committee on Reformatory and Industrial Schools*, Cd. 8939, H.M.S.O., 1913.

schools. They made many recommendations which reflected the disclosures of the Akbar affair. These included increased control by the Home Office, regulations for managers, an appeal to local authorities to involve themselves more in the establishment and management of these schools, improvements in the quality of senior staff, provisions for systematic medical care, and stringent regulations on punishment, industrial training, leisure activities and domestic arrangements. Their most controversial suggestions concerned the introduction of dual inspection of schools by Home Office and Board of Education inspectors and complex financial reforms. The schools welcomed many of the Committee's recommendations but expressed grave reservations about some of them and feared the proposed increase in central control.[1] The schools wanted discussion and some alterations to the proposals before legislation was prepared, but events overtook them.[2] The Home Office was clearly determined to introduce the recommended changes without additional authority and the schools were beginning to complain about 'the unseemly haste in introducing changes that are hateful' whilst delaying 'reforms that are eagerly desired'.[3] A few months later there were grumbles about the enforcement of the recommendations 'as though they were the law of the land' and that schools would need 'at least two extra clerks if they were to satisfy the newly-added demands of the Home Office' for returns and reports.[4] Although the new chief inspector who had been appointed in 1913 was popular and sympathetic to the schools he was determined to change them.[5]

[1] *Seeking and Saving* (vol. xviii, 1913, p. 378) referred to 'the two defective characteristics of an otherwise excellent report – over inspection and blindness to the special requirements of the schools'. The recommendations concerning administration are discussed in more detail under the headings of Home Office and voluntary management.

[2] A large deputation of managers and heads of schools met Home Office officials in October 1913 for discussions, *Seeking and Saving*, vol. xviii, 1913, pp. 434–58.

[3] *Seeking and Saving*, vol. xviii, 1914, p. 501.   [4] Ibid., p. 565.

[5] Russell attacked the prejudice against the schools in an article in the *Charity Organisations Review* (*Seeking and Saving*, vol. xvii, 1911, pp. 440–1) and wrote a sympathetic article in the *Evening News* (12 October 1912) but criticized them when he was guest of honour at a Social Union dinner a few months after his appointment (*Seeking and Saving*, vol. xviii, 1914, pp. 494–5).

A few months after the publication of the report a separate branch in the Home Office was formed to deal with the certified schools, juvenile courts, probation, cruelty to children and street-trading by children.[1] The war retarded progress somewhat. Although Russell was pushing for changes and improvements the schools were less co-operative because the war had made them more secure. Numbers were rising; from 1915 the schools accepted sub-contracts for munitions work[2] and a disproportionately large number of former inmates of the schools were in the armed forces, 4,000 were killed in action, 145 were commissioned and six were awarded the Victoria Cross.[3]

Russell died suddenly and Arthur Norris became chief inspector.[4] He was almost immediately involved in the problem of Homer Lane's Little Commonwealth[5] and was appointed chairman of a Departmental Committee on qualifications, pay and conditions of service of school staffs. This report was not published but it decided for Norris the changes he wanted to introduce. He told the schools that he wanted to change the education in the schools, that children were to be offered what a good working-class home offers, better classification, better transfer arrangements, provision for physically defective children and greater public interest in the schools.[6] His tone was imperious: 'There are certain things which I want you to do.'[7] Shortly afterwards, at a Social Union dinner, he told managers

[1] *Seeking and Saving*, vol. xviii, 1914, p. 493.

[2] *59th Report of the Chief Inspector of Reformatory and Industrial Schools*, Cd. 8367, H.M.S.O., 1916, p. 36.

[3] *First Report on the work of the Children's Branch*, H.M.S.O., 1923, p. 16.

[4] Russell died in April 1917 and Mr. A. Maxwell of the Children's Department Home Office acted as Chief Inspector until December 1917 when Norris took over.

[5] The 'official' closure of the Little Commonwealth held no hint of scandal. Lord Sandwich, its chairman, merely reported that they would close temporarily owing to 'difficult war conditions' (*Seeking and Saving*, vol. xx, 1918, p. 71), but some years later Sir Edward Troup, who was at the Home Office at the time, told magistrates that 'only mischief could come from listening to foolish people who had dabbled a little in the obscene publications of Freud and his School'. He also warned that psychoanalysis made girls indulge in sexual intercourse prematurely. See *Certified Schools Gazette*, vol. 17:3, 1923, p. 26.

[6] *Certified Schools Gazette*, vol. 12:4, 1919, pp. 39–48.

[7] Ibid., p. 44.

and superintendents: 'I have given you a great task to remodel your whole system.'[1]

There now began the most extraordinary period in the history of the schools. Committals to the schools declined so sharply that more than forty of them were closed.[2] Hostility to the schools in the courts and among penologists was unprecedented, and almost without exception those with powers of decision preferred to place a child continuously on probation rather than commit him to a certified school. The Home Office, mainly through its dynamic chief inspector, made increasing demands on the schools. For all that, the schools, with a non-reconviction rate of between 85 and 90 per cent, were more successful than at any other time before or since.

TABLE 2

Annual averages[3]

(Disposal of Convicted Children)

Years	Children sent to reformatories		Children placed on probation	
	No	%	No	%
1913–1919	1,375	3·11	5,438	12·04
1920–1924	630	2·01	4,962	16·09

Already in 1921 an editorial in the *Certified Schools Gazette* was demanding: 'Is it or is it not the real policy of the . . . Home Office . . . to kill the schools . . . ?'[4] At the same time the Howard League for Penal Reform weighed in viciously with a review of the unpublished report of the Departmental Committee of 1919 which showed, it was claimed, that children in these schools were no more than 'little factory hands in inefficient factories' staffed by ill-qualified officers. Norris was congratulated for his 'courage and audacity' in producing this 'most damning indictment of the privately managed, publicly financed certified

[1] *Certified Schools Gazette*, vol. 12:9, 1920, p. 104.
[2] *First Report Home Office Children's Branch*, H.M.S.O., 1923, p. 17.
[3] *First-Third Reports Home Office Children's Branch*, H.M.S.O., 1923–1925.
[4] *Certified Schools Gazette*, vol. 13:8, 1921, p. 94.

schools system we have yet seen'.[1] The *Gazette* was insistent in its challenge: 'The schools have just cause to complain of the complacency with which the Home Office have allowed them to be maligned.' They even warned that if the schools are indeed superfluous then this would make the children's branch equally superfluous.[2] Within a month they repeated their complaint: 'It cannot be too strongly emphasized that the certified schools are smarting badly from a sense of injustice and lack of appreciation. . . . They resent the persecution of misdirected opinion and now boldly challenge an investigation.'[3] The managers and superintendents met the women magistrates of the International Council of Women in January 1922 and pleaded for a better understanding of the schools and their function.[4] An article in the *Manchester Guardian* began thus: 'The feeling against the Certified Schools as a method of redeeming the juvenile delinquent is so widespread both among penal reformers and the relatives of the children themselves, that it is only fair to record any instance one encounters of apparent success in this direction.'[5] But at the Hertfordshire Assizes Mr. Justice Bray said that he did not like reformatories 'because I do constantly find that . . . old time offenders have begun their career in a reformatory'.[6] In all this upheaval the Home Office remained fairly detached. Whilst Norris and other senior members assured the schools of full support they did little to intervene publicly in defence of the schools. Home Office reports, while stressing the progress made by the schools, always underlined the existing shortcomings as well. Almost every report carried comments about the unjust criticisms the schools were subjected to,[7] but the schools themselves did not feel that they were given the support they felt entitled to.[8] It seemed to

[1] *Howard Journal*, 'Those Unreformed Reformatories', vol. 1:1, 1922, pp. 48–9.

[2] *Certified Schools Gazette*, vol. 14:11, p. 299.

[3] Ibid., 14:12, 1922, p. 310.

[4] Minutes of that meeting were kindly supplied to me by Mrs. M. F. Bligh, vice-president of the Council (1966).

[5] E. Sharp, writing about a visit to I. Ellis's school, 24 January 1923.

[6] *Certified Schools Gazette*, vol. 15:4, 1923, p. 63.

[7] Cf. *2nd Report*, 1924, p. 23; *3rd Report*, 1925, p. 23.

[8] 'The belief is hardening that the schools are being slowly disbanded (*Certified Schools Gazette*, vol. 17:5, 1924, p. 38). When I. Briggs published a

the schools that the Home Office was conspiring with magistrates and probation officers to get the schools closed.[1] In a desperate bid for understanding Ellis addressed a meeting of probation officers in Liverpool. He challenged the view that probation was cheaper or more successful than residential treatment and suggested that co-operation and mutual understanding were the proper approach for people who shared a common desire to help the 'erring child'.[2]

The schools were fully justified in wondering whether their continued existence could be taken for granted. In 1925, committals to reformatories represented only a very small fraction of convicted children whilst a substantial number were placed on probation.[3] Sidney Harris, the head of the Children's Department of the Home Office, offered four reasons for the fall in committals. First, he listed the reluctance of local authorities to pay; secondly, the effect of improved education; thirdly, the 'dole' which made it possible to keep the families of the unemployed together, and, finally, the impact of probation.[4] As might be expected those children who were sent to reformatories were more difficult than most[5] and it is not easy to see how the schools maintained such a high success rate under such trying conditions. One explanation might be the relative attitudes in the institution and its environment. Thus, while the schools were to some extent rigid and regimented they felt strongly for their inmates, partly because that was their

---

scathing attack (*Reformatory Reform*, London, Longmans, 1924) on the schools in which he had been an inmate around 1911–1913, the schools were annoyed that the Home Office had refused him permission to re-visit schools at the time he wrote his book. He was then a university graduate (*Certified Schools Gazette*, vol. 19:4, 1925, p. 13).

[1] *Certified Schools Gazette*, vol. 18:8, 1924, pp. 71–2.

[2] *Seeking and Saving*, vol. xxv, 1925, pp. 232–43.

[3] 26 per cent of the children found guilty of offences in 1925 were placed on probation. 2·4 per cent were committed to reformatories (*Departmental Committee*, 1927, p. 13). Even advertisers reacted to this. Many issues of the *Certified Schools Gazette* at this time had half their advertising space blank.

[4] *Certified Schools Gazette*, vol. 18:10, 1924, p. 94, but the Home Secretary thought that the fall in admissions was due to 'the improvement in the moral tone and social well-being of the country' (*Seeking and Saving*, vol. xxvi, 1926, p. 87).

[5] Cf. *Third Report on the Work of the Children's Branch*, 1925, p. 26, and *Fourth Report on the Work of the Children's Branch*, 1928, p. 32.

professional concern and partly because they felt themselves to be on trial and under public scrutiny. This concern was undoubtedly transmitted to the children and offered them a sense of security and belonging. In the wider community, however, for all the liberal spirit which frowned on institutional treatment, conditions were very different.

Unemployment was high, opportunities for work and leisure were limited and not generally regarded as an individual's right. To the extent that survival depended on conformity institutions were a better training ground than they are today when schools may be more demanding than society.

A new Departmental Committee, so long and so frequently called for by the schools, was finally appointed and began its deliberations in 1925. But Norris discontinued his annual reports and this must have been another severe blow to the schools who were, by now, almost completely dependent on the Home Office for justifying their existence.[1] The fact that no one connected with the schools was appointed to the new committee was also deplored. The Home Office now issued a circular suggesting that the title of superintendent be dropped as being too reminiscent of prisons. Henceforth headmaster or matron were to be used.[2] In yet another bid for better understanding the National Association of Reformatory and Industrial schools arranged a meeting with the National Association of Probation Officers where co-operation was the main theme.[3] A further meeting was held under the auspices of the Home Office in March 1926 at which it was agreed that probation officers (instead of police escorts) should take committed children to the schools and use this opportunity to get to know the schools.[4]

When the Departmental Committee reported in 1927[5] they had relatively little to say or recommend on the certified

---

[1] An editorial in the *Certified Schools Gazette* hailed the Report for 1924 as 'the best report aimed to cure past ills' (vol. 18:12, 1924, pp. 113–15).

[2] *Certified Schools Gazette*, vol. 19:7, 1925, pp. 37–8.

[3] The meeting was held on 25 November 1925, see *Certified Schools Gazette*, vol. 20:4, 1926, p. 40.

[4] *Seeking and Saving*, vol. xxv, 1926, pp. 98–106 and 117–29.

[5] *Report of the Departmental Committee on the Treatment of Young Offenders*, Cmd. 2831, H.M.S.O. 1927.

schools.[1] Schools were to abolish the names Reformatory and Industrial and be known as Approved Schools. Apart from some minor provisions, they recommended that managers be deprived of the right to refuse admission to a child sent by a court, a proposal that was unanimously (albeit unsuccessfully) rejected by the managers.[2] The Committee thought that the schools were better than at any other time in their history. They welcomed the fall in admissions as a healthy sign but recognized the need for such institutions for certain children.[3] The various changes which had been introduced since 1913 were codified in the Acts of 1932 and 1933[4] and the pattern of the schools was firmly set.

The real importance of the Report of 1927 lay in its final abolition of any distinction between the two types of school, thus completing a process first begun by the Committee of 1896. By defining the catchment of these schools 'all classes of neglected and delinquent children',[5] an implicit denial of specific treatment for young offenders in such schools was put forward which made the recent government proposals of 1965 possible, but which, at the same time, made it impossible for the schools to define an aim and purpose for themselves which could take account of their dual function in caring under one roof and by one and the same method, for children who need help and children who need correction.[6] But it was not really the Report of 1927 which set the pattern. A year previously Norris had summoned the managers and heads of schools to a conference. He would not allow minutes to be kept and addressed the gathering decisively, praising, blaming, demanding changes.[7] For Norris had achieved complete and unchallenged mastery over the schools. Henceforth all the schools would accept his undisputed leadership and entered a state of

---

[1] Thus the Report devoted twice as much space to a discussion of Borstals as it did on certified schools.

[2] *Seeking and Saving*, vol. xxviii, 1928, p. 2.

[3] *Report*, 1927, p. 71.

[4] 23 & 23 Geo. V, c.46 and 23 Geo. V, c.12.

[5] *Report*, 1927, p. 125.

[6] See especially *Report of the Care of Children Committee*, Cmd. 6922, H.M.S.O., 1946 (Curtis Committee), para. 498, pp. 170–1.

[7] *Seeking and Saving*, vol. xxvi, 1926, pp. 280–1.

dependency on the Home Office which persisted even when it withdrew positive leadership from the schools when Norris retired.[1]

[1] It is interesting to note that Norris's dynamic influence coincided with Alex Paterson's leadership of Borstals. See Roger Hood, *Borstals Re-Assessed*, London, Heinemann, 1965, esp. p. 32.

Chapter 3

Policy Makers: Past and Present

It is a measure of the success as well as the failure of approved schools that they do not appear to have changed very much since the turbulent days of the 1920s. Some changes have occurred. Systematic classification was introduced in 1942 with the establishment of Aycliffe School.[1] Three special (closed) units for persistent absconders were introduced between 1964–1966,[2] and attempts have been made to introduce modern remedial methods in some schools.[3] Standards of care and training for staff have steadily improved, but success rates have fallen and now stand at 38 per cent.[4] Over the past thirty years there have been attacks in newspapers and in the courts, there have been criticisms and enquiries following disturbances in some schools. The prejudice against the schools displayed by probation officers in the 1920s is still encountered amongst social workers today, but the great debates have been largely muted, the schools have become more of a 'silent service'.[5]

In the Curtis Committee Report of 1946, approved schools came out rather well and it is worth noting that that Committee found no real difference between schools managed by local

[1] See J. Gittins, *Approved School Boys*, H.M.S.O., 1952.

[2] *Report – Children's Department*, 1964–1966, H.M.S.O., 1967, p. 53.

[3] These include group work and 'therapeutic communities'. While it is not suggested that these experiments are not working they have yet to have a visible influence on the system as a whole.

[4] *Report*, 1964–1966, op. cit., p. 51.

[5] This is borne out by the apparent reluctance of the schools to publish what is probably the most valuable material produced by them in recent years, namely the reports of review meetings between classifying and training schools.

95

authorities and those managed by private individuals.[1] In this study we will have to restrict ourselves to developments in the Home Office and voluntary management which will also illustrate how the schools have fared since the days of Arthur Norris.

There is however one point which should be mentioned because it demonstrates how far the schools regard themselves to have moved from their original object of training young offenders. In 1921, when admissions were falling and schools were being closed, the superintendents of schools were greatly concerned about the security of tenure of members of staff. A deputation went to the Home Office and suggested that unwanted reformatories might be used as 'mild Borstals'.[2] The same situation arose in the early 1950s. Numbers were falling and the Home Office began to close some of the approved schools. In 1955 the Association of Headmasters produced a pamphlet in which they deplored this situation, pleaded for security of tenure for staff, and suggested that unwanted approved schools might be used as residential units for mentally or emotionally handicapped children and staffed by the same personnel.[3]

I VOLUNTARY MANAGEMENT

The experiences of the prototypal institutions were repeated in the management of later institutions. The Philanthropic had been set up as a charitable organization and, as we have seen, floundered somewhat inefficiently until the arrival of Sydney Turner. Although technically an employee of the managing committee, he was nevertheless able to sit at their meetings as a social equal. It is quite possible that the committee's insistence on always choosing a clergyman to head the Philanthropic may

[1] There has, however, been some pressure from therapeutically orientated workers to resolve the ambiguous position of approved schools as punitive and child-care institutions, and as training and treatment units. See for example M. Schmideberg, *Children in Need*, London, Allen & Unwin, 1948, ch. II.

[2] *Certified Schools Gazette*, vol. 13:8, pp. 96–9.

[3] Assocation of Headmasters, Headmistresses and Matrons of approved schools. Technical Sub-Committee Monograph No. 7, *Approved Schools and the Future*, 1955, esp. pp. 6–7.

have been based on this need to find an officer whose social position was close to that of other members. In the case of Parkhurst prison, Visitors acted as a committee of management but because they were all paid government servants they were unacceptable to Victorian society as people able to do good in their own right.

The leaders of the reformatory school movement wanted something better and more effective than either of these alternatives. Mary Carpenter argued the case for the voluntary manager.[1] In her view, it was the duty of the State to assume full responsibility for those children whose parents had failed them and in this group she included orphaned, destitute and convicted children. The State should delegate parental responsibility to those who could assume it, and carry out strict inspections to see that this was done. She justified this argument by saying that such a system would be

... the best means of supplying to the child the parental relation, [and] that every inducement should be held out to lead individuals or individual bodies ... to establish such institutions, where the child might be, in a measure, restored to the natural condition of a family and brought under individual influence. The State should however always exercise a close inspection on such institutions.[2]

She suggested that the State should give managers sufficient powers to exercise 'correctional discipline' over offenders but also demanded the appointment of inspectors '. . . who shall frequently examine the working and management of the school and its reformatory effect on the children. . .'.[3] Although Mary Carpenter had very little experience of reformatory management when she put forward these ideas, they became binding throughout the nineteenth century and are one of the main factors underlying the idea of voluntary management today. After 1854 many institutions were established by men imbued with the ideals of the reformatory school movement, who were at the same time people of power and position in their communities. At a meeting of managers at Hardwick in 1861 almost all of those present were magistrates 'of some weight and

---

[1] Mary Carpenter, *Juvenile Delinquents – Their Condition and Treatment* 1853, p. 377.
[2] Ibid., p. 378.   [3] Ibid., p. 379.

experience in their own communities' and five were chairmen of quarter sessions. All were closely concerned with the prevention and treatment of crime in their areas.[1] They were men who accepted full responsibility for their work and considered it only right that their institutions be '. . . judged not by the polish of . . . floors or the goodness of . . . dinners, but by the after life of those who had left the school and by the rarity of those who required its treatment'.[2]

Unfortunately, the idealistic position of the great leaders in the movement could not be maintained and upheld throughout the country, as more and more men involved themselves in the management of reformatories. Apart from the unavoidable routinization of what were once conceived as sacred duties, there were bound to be newcomers to the work whose interest may have been less altruistic, whose understanding of the problem was less comprehensive and whose sympathy with the tasks was less sincere. While the early pioneers often spent a considerable amount of time daily or weekly in their reformatories and with the youngsters, many others with conflicting commitments were less keen, less frequently seen, and content to rely on their staff to do the things that had to be done. Another unavoidable consequence of the spread of diverse types of institutions was that the Home Office inspectorate, so strongly advocated and so greatly welcomed by early pioneers, was bound to clash with managers whose work it regarded as unsatisfactory. At first the inspectors were somewhat circumspect in their handling of managers and only rarely commented directly on their work. In 1861, Turner remarked of one school that he thought its staff would be more effective if they did not depend quite so much on the assistance of the managers.[3] In 1867 when Turner commented on the poor schooling provided in many reformatories, he was told by the managers that '. . . the business of a reformatory is to correct rather than instruct, and that the reform of temper and habits, development of industry and exercise of self-control are what they have to aim at. . .'.[4] In the same year

[1] T. Berwick, I. L. Baker, in *War with Crime*, edited by H. Phillips and E. Verney, London, 1889, p. 212.
[2] Ibid., p. 225.
[3] *Fourth Report. Inspector of Reformatories and Industrial Schools*, 1861, p. 47.
[4] *Tenth Report. Inspector of Reformatories and Industrial Schools*, 1867, p. 8.

there was also a report of the manager of one reformatory who made up annual deficits in the school budget from his own resources.[1] To some extent the inspectors' hesitation in openly criticizing, at any rate the first generation of managers, was due to a reluctance to accept detailed government control. This can be illustrated from a report in 1868:

the managers of this reformatory resigned their certificate in October in consequence of the discharge, by order of the Secretary of State, of a girl who they were of opinion should be retained . . . the managers acted no doubt from a conviction that their authority was unduly interfered with. . . .[2]

With the passing of the great pioneers and the growth of mechanical and regimented institutions in the last quarter of the century, however, criticism of the managers by the inspectorate took on a different tone. In 1880 the inspector wrote: 'I gave the managers to understand that more time and attention must be given to the education of girls. . . .'[3] Another report stated that 'the present arrangements are thoroughly unsatisfactory and this has been explained to the managers fully and repeatedly'.[4]

The Royal Commission of 1884 were characteristically ambivalent about what they called 'an unofficial body of governors' and made their criticism more by implication than by a straightforward assessment of the situation. They approved of voluntary management and wanted to interfere as little as possible with it. They also thought that voluntary management schools were better than those managed by local authorities and school boards. They were against central government control for the following reasons:

1 Children needed the personal care of voluntary managers.
2 The schools were so scattered that central administration was thought to be impossible.

[1] Ibid., p. 58.
[2] *Eleventh Report. Inspector of Reformatories and Industrial Schools*, 1868, p. 53.
[3] *Twenty-third Report. Inspector of Reformatories and Industrial Schools*, 1880, p. 92.
[4] *Twenty-sixth Report. Inspector of Reformatories and Industrial Schools*, 1883, p. 62.

3 Voluntary management brought voluntary subscriptions to help finance the schools.

4 The religious zeal of voluntary managers must not be lost.

Even so their recommendations to the inspectorate showed that certain weaknesses in voluntary management had become well established. They urged that inspection should ensure that 'local management is a reality', that committees meet regularly and exercise due supervision and control over superintendents. These recommendations demanded less than a circular from the Home Office inspectorate in 1881 which laid down as fixed duties for managers that they have monthly meetings, exercise vigilant personal supervision and have at least one weekly visit by a manager to the school. The commission warned that weak management could easily lead to disorder and that the resultant uproar was harmful to all schools. They also stated that too many schools, including girls' schools, had no women managers.[1]

In a discussion of voluntary management, the Departmental Committee of 1896 made a careful analysis of what they regarded as the main weaknesses of the system. They described five main weaknesses; large schools cheaply administered, the prolonged detention of children, the choice of industrial employments which were profitable to the school rather than instructive for the children, refusal to transfer children to school ships when their interest required it, and the systematic and unnecessary return of children to friends (i.e. home). The Committee felt that these weaknesses could be eliminated under a system of state administration, but they went on to say that: 'the personal interest of individuals is so invaluable, whenever it exists that . . . voluntary management ought on no account to be superseded'. There is a hint in the report that perhaps a compromise solution would ultimately be best, placing schools under local authorities and so maintaining the main advantages of voluntary management with the efficiency, security, and higher standards of governmental administration.[2]

[1] *Report of the Royal Commission on Reformatories and Industrial Schools*, 1884, printed as Appendix VIII to the *Report of the Departmental Committee of 1896*, para. 6–9, pp. 217–18.

[2] *Report of the Departmental Committee on Reformatories and Industrial Schools*, 1896, para. 201, pp. 105–6.

The managers themselves were fully aware of the considerable divergencies of standards between schools and the desultory modes of management exercised in some of them. It seems likely that the steady rise to growing and increased prominence of the superintendents of institutions was due in some instances to schools whose management committees were so ineffective that the schools could only survive if they had a strong superintendent; in others, as in the case of the Philanthropic, it was the appearance of strong and efficient superintendents that caused many management committees to give up more and more of their powers and responsibilities. Such an explanation was suggested by Martin, who warned managers that, where an institution was working well under a good superintendent, managers might be inclined to leave well alone but that this would be a very dangerous thing to do. Managers should remember that all staff needed encouragement, sympathy, and advice because residential work was very monotonous. Such help could only be offered by someone who clearly understood the problems involved by frequent visits to the institution. He also thought that the children were very conscious of the managers' interest in them and he regarded this as part of the treatment process. He added that where residential workers expressed a preference for being 'left alone' this would be due to the indifference managers had shown towards the work.[1] Another factor in elevating superintendents arose from the practice in a few schools of combining the post of superintendent with that of manager, as a 'resident governor' or lady superintendent. This was more likely in the smaller schools.

At the turn of the century, voluntary management was so firmly entrenched that its functions were rarely discussed. Those in favour of the *status quo* tended to defend their position by pointing to good schools where management worked well, and those who were against the system, or wanted to be critical of it, drew attention to bad schools where management was inefficient or ineffective. Since both sides argued from the particular to the general, no argument was ever conclusive and this type of discussion has moved backwards and forwards ever since.

[1] T. H. Martin, 'Co-operation between the Hon. Managers and the Workers in Institutions', *Reformatory and Refuge Union Journal*, vol. xiii, 1897, pp. 39–40.

The Departmental Committee of 1913 tried to take a positive view of management. They were more concerned to show what a good manager did than to elaborate on details of management failure. Yet even here the implied criticism was quite clear. The best managers, they said, visit schools frequently, know the children in them personally, know the working of the institution and help and stimulate the staff. Where management was not efficient, the Committee felt that the Home Office should intervene. They again pointed out that very few schools had women managers and recommended that committees of management should meet at least once a quarter, that at least one manager should visit the school every month, and that the Home Office should have power to nominate one manager to each school committee.[1] They also drew attention to the very important fact that most voluntary schools were owned, or the property was held in trust, by managers and that this might complicate any widespread change without considerable legal preparations.[2] In the same year that the Committee published its report Barnett[3] published her book on young delinquents; the first, and for over fifty years the only, university-based assessment of the schools.[4] She was very critical of managers and complained that there were very few women managers,[5] that methods of selecting managers should be changed and that managers were distant and superior with the children in their care and should try to become real friends to them.[6] She found most committees consisted of magistrates, doctors, clergymen, retired officers, and county and city magnates.[7]

Norris thought that managers varied as much as the schools themselves. Some took immense interest in their work while others rarely entered the schools; knew little of what went on inside them; held meetings fifty miles from the schools; rarely or never visited similar schools or showed the slightest interest in how others were coping with similar problems.[8] He did not

---

[1] This recommendation was implemented by the Criminal Justice Act, 1961.

[2] *Report of the Departmental Committee on Reformatory and Industrial Schools*, Cd. 6838, 1913, pp. 18–19.

[3] Mary G. Barnett, *Young Delinquents*, London, 1913.

[4] Gordon Rose's *Schools for Young Offenders*, London, 1967, was the second.

[5] Barnett, op. cit., p. 42.   [6] Ibid., p. 43.   [7] Ibid., p. 42.

[8] A. H. Norris, 'The Certified Reformatory and Industrial Schools', *Seeking and Saving*, vol. xxii, 1922, pp. 13–22.

want to abolish voluntary management but to improve it.

When the managers of a school are active and keenly interested in their school the voluntary system can probably secure better results than any other. Its defects become apparent when the Committee of Management is weak, narrow in outlook or unprogressive. It is so easy for a body of this kind, when perhaps changes are only rarely made in its personnel, to grow weary of well-doing, or having reached a certain standard of development to live on its past achievement. There is always need of new blood in any committee, however able and keen its members, and it would be well if in some cases the experience and wisdom of age could be supplemented by the enthusiasm and freshness of youth. Most Committees of Management would be improved by new recruits from time to time.[1]

The effect of the hostile criticism which was directed at the reformatory and industrial schools generally and at the managers, led to some extent to a sense of isolation, but it also drew the managers closer together and on 23 November 1921 they formed an Association of Voluntary Managers and defined their objects as follows:

1 To promote intercourse and exchange of views between managers.
2 To make general representation to authorities on matters of policy, administration, finance and innovations in schools.
3 To preserve the voluntary system.
4 To co-operate, when advisable, with the Society of Superintendents and the National Association of Reformatory and Industrial Schools.
5 Any other matters related to the efficiency and welfare of the schools, inmates and staff.

The first action of the new association was to send a letter to the Home Secretary in which they protested that magistrates put too many children on probation and in which they asked for freedom to dispose of maintenance grants after the Home Office had approved their estimates. Both points were rejected by the Home Office.[2] There was also a growing concern amongst the managers over the increasing part local authorities

[1] *Home Office Report on the Work of the Children's Branch*, H.M.S.O., 1923, p. 23.
[2] *Seeking and Saving*, vol. xxii, 1922, pp. 30–32.

were beginning to play in the administration of child welfare. In 1921 there was a bitter attack on the London County Council for assuming managerial functions over licensing children from industrial schools. The report spoke of an 'almost clandestine conspiracy [between the L.C.C. and Home Office] to relegate the managers to the background' in favour of 'bureaucratic administration'.[1]

This fear was also expressed in a recorded public discussion on the voluntary principle. Since this principle lies at the heart of the system it may be convenient here to look at it in a little more detail. The idea of the early Victorian pioneers, as explained by Mary Carpenter, was simple and logical. The children to be dealt with were children whose parents, for one reason or another, had failed them. Parents were seen not only as care-givers but, more important, as the primary socialization agents, the adults who implant in children the norms and values of the society into which they were being reared. Where parents failed, the State must assume responsibility for the children, but it was not considered possible that parental function could be exercised directly, because the State was seen essentially as an administrative instrument and not as an educational or humanitarian agency. The State would therefore delegate the role of parent to those men and women who were imbued with a devotion to the norms and values of their society which they would transmit to the children on behalf of the State, and in lieu of the parents. It was this idea that gave rise to the legal concept of managers standing *in loco parentis* to the children in reformatory and industrial schools. Without such an explicit socializing function the concept of *in loco parentis* and the legal powers that go with it are difficult to justify.

Throughout the nineteenth century there was no private or governmental agency which could, in any way, be regarded as an alternative body in carrying out these functions, and management felt secure. So secure, in fact, that they were willing and able to defy both government and public opinion on the question of the previous imprisonment of children. But we have already seen that towards the end of the nineteenth century the superintendents were becoming more professional and influential in the management of schools. Local authorities

[1] *Seeking and Saving*, vol. xxi, 1921, pp. 111–12.

assumed control over an increasing number of industrial schools and thereby created an entirely new type of voluntary manager, and the Home Office, by assuming an ever-increasing control over the functions and duties of voluntary managers, tended to influence the type of person who would be likely to devote himself to this kind of social work.[1] A growing emphasis in reformatory work concentrated more on the welfare of children and on emotional maturity than on the dubious claims by managers to social superiority derived from social class, and on the technical and mechanical preparation of children for employment and social conformity. Although this process was a very slow one, it steadily undermined the original role of voluntary managers as spokesmen and representatives of their communities, and the general feeling that the member of one social class had an absolute right to reject the values of another class and superimpose his own became less and less accepted. Finally, the attitude to, and the participation of, the parents of the children in the schools has also undergone a slow but steady change. The total, almost violent, rejection of them by people like Mary Carpenter[2] has gradually given way to an increasing recognition of the fact that even a socially unacceptable parent will be of great emotional importance to his child. The attitude that the best way to help a child from a poor background is to separate it completely and permanently from that background (e.g. by emigration) has been replaced today by the principle that children who must go into approved schools should, where possible, go to schools that are nearest their home, where maximum contact between parent and child can be maintained and even increased by the school.[3]

It is a matter of some interest that during the public discussion on the voluntary principle which took place in 1921[4] most

---

[1] This influence may have worked in a largely negative sense by alienating strong and vigorous reformers.

[2] 'It is not so much poverty which fills our prisons with young criminals, as the vicious conduct and culpable neglect of parents.' Mary Carpenter in *Juvenile Delinquents – Their Condition and Treatment*, London 1853, p. 152.

[3] This is now often described as 'geographical allocation', cf. *Aycliffe 1967*, A Report on the Classifying School, p. 50.

[4] M. A. Spielman, 'The Importance of the Preservation of the Voluntary Principle in Child Saving and Rescue Work', *Reformatory and Refuge Union Conference Report*, London, 1921, pp. 5–8. Discussion, pp. 8–26.

of the participants, although they argued strongly and emotionally, never defined what they meant or wanted by this, but based their arguments on what they feared or did not want. The discussion was initiated by Spielman, a former inspector in the Home Office, who claimed that 'the principle of voluntary management . . . is being seriously assailed. . .'. He described the principle as 'voluntary management in the hands of men and women to whom the work is of very special value and interest, who give time and labour, who bring devotion, love, self-sacrifice and spirituality to individual needs in these institutions'. He claimed that the State could not conceivably act *in loco parentis*, and that neither local authority nor paid officials could satisfy the individual needs of children. He agreed that bad voluntary managers should be replaced but claimed that there was no evidence that there were any. He further maintained that under 'State managers' there would be endless delays and frequent staff changes and from local authority managers 'fitness could scarcely be expected'. Spielman was strongly supported by the Principal of the National Children's Homes who claimed that 'people do not and will not give their services to the State'. He warned that State management would lead to stiff and unbending standardization; to dead, level, mediocrity; to a reduction of children into types; to a destruction of individuality; that the State would only provide officials and not parental figures and that paid officials had no sympathy or real interest in those they dealt with. Ellis also supported Spielman by claiming that some people who knew nothing about it had called for the abolition of voluntary management.

The Chief Inspector of the Home Office tried to reassure the voluntary managers by saying that although he thought some modifications to the system were needed, there was no question of abolition. He could not resist the opportunity to voice some criticisms and complained that managers were very reluctant to accept new people on their boards and spoke of three committees where the average age was over seventy. Sir Harry Stephens of the L.C.C. rejected the thesis that local authorities or paid officials were any less valuable than voluntary managers. He thought that a large body like the L.C.C. was able to gather invaluable experience on many aspects of institutional management which they could then apply for the benefit of many institutions.

The most reasoned contribution came from Margery Fry. She suggested that if there was a dispute about managers it was more about how they should be appointed and what their function should be rather than whether or not they should exist at all. She insisted that the parental role in an institution was played by the paid staff and not by the managers, but saw a valuable function for voluntary managers, who would see that public money was spent properly, help schools in emergencies, and appoint and control staff. She thought that public management would unify the school system and strongly denied that public servants were incapable of love, devotion and sympathy.[1]

The overtones of defensiveness during that meeting were justified by Spielman, who claimed that a bill had been prepared by the government to transfer school management from voluntary to state managers. In spite of reassurances from the Chief Inspector, the meeting passed a resolution by an overwhelming majority, that the voluntary principle was essential to the well-being of institutions.[2]

Although the voluntary principle continues to be reiterated and supported, no serious attempt has been made to re-evaluate it or to define it in the context of prevailing conditions. Thus, the Association of Approved School Heads in their evidence to the Ingleby Committee recommended the continuance of voluntary management without, however, giving any reasoned arguments in its favour.[3] In their evidence to the Royal Commission on the Penal System the managers and headmasters urged that voluntary management should be retained because it gave the schools 'a degree of independence that is valuable,

[1] She adopted a more traditional view of managers in later years but insisted that they should have real knowledge of child-care problems. See M. Fry, *Arms of the Law*, London, 1951, p. 130.

[2] Spielman, op. cit., p. 25. Spielman's reference to a bill probably referred to Bill 31 (II Geo. V.), March 1921, which made some minor amendments to the Children's Act of 1908, all of a financial nature and including a provision which repealed a clause limiting the obligations of local authorities with respect to maintenance of children in institutions (Sect. 3).

[3] Association of Headmasters, Headmistresses and Matrons of Approved Schools, *Evidence for Presentation to the Ingleby Committee*, Technical Sub-Committee Monograph No. 8, 1957, p. 22.

permitting innovation and unique experimentation', but they added that they would like to see representatives of statutory bodies on committees.[1] The White Paper of 1965 expressed appreciation and support of 'voluntary effort' but did not justify its continuance.[2] In a comment on the White Paper the Joint Approved School Associations went so far as to suggest that voluntary management 'has as many disadvantages as advantages' and stated as the main advantages (a) that people interested only in school management but not local politics could be included as managers [presumably in Local Authority schools], and (b) that voluntary action 'expresses the needs of minorities'.[3] One group of managers argued their case before a group of M.P.s and put forward five points:

1 Voluntary managers give schools an invaluable link with local communities.
2 They accept office because they are interested in social work.
3 They have and devote more time to the needs of children.
4 They often specialize in their fields and can thus contribute in depth.
5 They often bring a religious or philanthropic orientation to the work.[4]

It is clear from these recent pronouncements that there is no real unity of view on the nature and value of the voluntary principle, and that the most recent arguments do not defend voluntary management as such but *ad hoc* voluntary management against voluntary management by politically-oriented, elected local councillors serving as managers on local authority committees.

In spite of yet another attack on voluntary management by

[1] Association of Managers of Approved Schools, and Association of Headmasters, Headmistresses and Matrons of Approved Schools, *Evidence for presentation to the Royal Commission on the Penal System*, 1965, p. 8.

[2] *The Child, The Family and the Young Offender*, Cmnd. 2742, H.M.S.O., 1965, para. 44, pp. 12–13.

[3] Associations of Managers – Headmasters, Headmistresses and Matrons of Approved Schools and the National Association of Approved School Staffs, *Observations on the White Paper, The Child, The Family and the Young Offender*, 1966, pp. 13–14.

[4] Northumberland and Durham Branch of the Association of Approved School Managers – Statement for Meeting with Socialist Members of Parliament, May 12th 1965 (mimeographed), pp. 2.

Chief Inspector Norris, who claimed that where institutions failed, this was due to the 'weakness of a committee which had ceased to function, where management was delegated to an inefficient staff',[1] the Departmental Committee of 1927 could see no reason for a fundamental change in management, and thought that the voluntary principle was justified by good committees. However, because funds now came largely from public sources, greater Home Office control was 'right and inevitable'.[2]

In 1923 the Home Office had published model rules for managers and these were supported by the Departmental Committee.[3] This reaffirmation quietened the discussions and criticisms, and for a time there was no comment on managers apart from a brief article in 1941 which complained of too much Home Office control and argued that managers were necessary to prevent a single person from assuming responsibility for all aspects of institutional administration.[4]

The era of quiet co-operation between the Home Office, managers, and staffs of approved schools was[5] shattered abruptly in 1947 when some boys at the Standon Farm Approved School shot a member of the staff and absconded. In the resultant enquiry some serious faults in the management system were brought to light:[6]

1 The School, which was situated some 12 miles north of Stafford and owned by a religious society, had been managed from London over the previous eight years (p. 9).

2 Although Rule 4 of the 1933 Approved School Rules stipulated that boys' schools must have at least two women managers, the committee included only one woman (p. 10).

3 Managers left licensing to the Headmaster (p. 16).

The boys in the school were very resentful about licensing

[1] A. H. Norris, 'The Management of Homes and Responsibilities of Committees', *Reformatory and Refuge Union Conference Report*, Liverpool, 1927, pp. 114–121.

[2] *Report of the Departmental Committee on the Treatment of Young Offenders*, Cmd. 2831, 1927, pp. 78–79.

[3] *Second Report – Children's Branch – Home Office*, 1924, Appendix II.

[4] 'Are Managers Really Necessary?', *Approved Schools Gazette*, 35:9, 1941, pp. 189–190.

[5] Cf. M. M. Simmons, *Making Citizens*, London, H.M.S.O., 1946, p. 10.

[6] *Report of the Committee of Enquiry into the conduct of Standon Farm Approved Schools*, Report of Enquiry, Cmnd. 937, 1960.

(p. 10), and the recommendations in the report leave no doubt about the unsatisfactory management system they found in the school (pp. 27–29). Whatever the effect of this incident and its consequences may have been, another report on a serious breakdown in an approved school, again singled out similarly unsatisfactory conditions related to management, notably the question of licensing.[1] The Ingleby Committee, which also reported in 1960,[2] also made many recommendations of which perhaps the most significant was the suggestion that managers should be given general guidance on 'the aims and purposes of Approved Schools and the responsibilities and functions of managers'.[3]

Already before the Ingleby Committee recommended that the Home Office should do something to acquaint managers with their duties and responsibilities in relation to approved schools, some attempts had been made by senior members of the Home Office to re-state some of the ideas which lay behind the system of approved school management. Thus Gwynn, in an address to managers, pointed out that they were responsible for the custody, training and licensing of children and that it was also their duty to see that public money was being spent to the best advantage. He thought that managers should try to special-ize in the various aspects of approved school work and suggested the need to attract young and, if possible, professional people into the work. He explained that managing an approved school covered a much wider area of activity than being a governor of an ordinary school.[4] In the following year Miss P. Hornsby-Smith emphasized the Home Office's approval of the idea of voluntary management: 'I revel in claiming that one of the greatest strengths of the approved school system lies in the diversity of the schools themselves. If ever a day comes when state officials supersede the great voluntary bodies of this country then the welfare services will be both thinner and

[1] V. Durand, *Disturbances at the Carlton Approved School – Report of Enquiry*, Cmnd. 937, 1960.
[2] *Report of the Committee on Children and Young Persons*, Cmnd. 1191, 1960, paras. 435–440, pp. 125–126.
[3] Op. cit., para. 440, p. 126.
[4] E. H. Gwynn (Under-Secretary of State, Home Office), 'Responsibilites of Managers', *Approved Schools Gazette*, 50:6, 1956, p. 195.

poorer.' She also summarized the duties of managers.[1] The Ingleby proposal was realized with the preparation of a handbook for approved school managers, perhaps one of the best compilations on the administration and function of approved schools to have been produced, certainly within the last thirty years, which for some unknown reason was never made available to the public at large by the Home Office.[2] The managers themselves very rarely commented in any depth or detail on the work they were doing, although occasional criticisms and memoranda were produced by the Managers' Association, usually to comment on a topical issue on which they felt strongly. For example, when the Home Office published a report on the non-residential treatment of offenders, the managers responded by pointing out in a memorandum that residential training is too often used as a last resort, that children who have experienced many forms of treatment before coming to an approved school often show a contempt for the law and that frequent probation is bad and makes approved school training more difficult.[3] Again in 1965 the Managers' Association made a vigorous attack on the prevailing custom in the Home Office of publishing annual success figures for approved schools. They challenged the meaningfulness of these figures and urged that, though they were not opposed to any form of evaluation of their work, they objected most strongly to success rates being used as a measure of success when such rates were no more than a 'twisted yardstick'.[4] From individual managers there is not very much that might be regarded as contributing to the problems of voluntary management. Ford has described some aspects at a personal level[5] and a useful and interesting

[1] P. Hornsby-Smith (Under-Secretary of State, Home Office), 'Address to the Association of Managers', *Approved Schools Gazette*, 51:6, 1957, pp. 211–214.

[2] Home Office, *A Handbook for Managers of Approved Schools*. Printed for private circulation, November 1961.

[3] 'Non-Residential Treatment of Offenders', Memorandum by the Association of Managers of Approved Schools, *Approved Schools Gazette*, 55:7, 1961, pp. 295–296.

[4] D. T. Cowan, The Managers' Association, *Approved Schools Gazette*, 59:8, 1965, pp. 338–339.

[5] D. Ford, *The Delinquent Child and the Community*, London, Constable, 1957, pp. 104–109.

paper was published by T. F. Tucker in 1961.[1] Adams (then a headmaster) prepared a brief survey of management in this century.[2] The most substantial review of approved schools in general but also of problems of management was the book by Gordon Rose.[3] In discussing managers, Rose is on the whole hostile to the concept and sees only little value in the perpetuation of the system. He provides no evidence, however, for many of the criticisms he makes. He thought that managers might have some use in the prevention of ill-treatment of children (p. 221) but only limited use as links with local communities (p. 223). He did not think that they were qualified to exercise the power of release properly (p. 223) and thought that inspectors were better able to control and supervise the activities of headmasters (p. 224). Managers had really nothing to contribute on the question of individual treatment (p. 224). He saw the real function of managers in that they owned the schools and that they could contribute to the general management of schools (p. 225) but felt that reforms were necessary, particularly in the provision of instruments of management by the Home Office, making firm rules concerning the duration of the appointment of managers, age of retirement, and redefinition of function.

In the course of time, therefore, the managers who were originally the trend-setters, the idealists, the reformers, the people who conceptualized and activated the various forms of treatment for destitute and delinquent children had been reduced to a position where it was necessary for an official report to advise that they should be told of their functions and their responsibilities or, to put it bluntly, they should be told what the schools they were managing were for. This would appear to be a sad reflection on the managers and might be regarded as both unfair and condemnatory if it were not for the fact that the changes which have been made in the respective roles and functions of the Home Office, the managers and the headmasters, have been so complex, so piecemeal and so arbit-

[1] T. F. Tucker, 'The Role of a Manager', *Approved Schools Gazette*, 55:4, 1961, pp. 128–32.

[2] R. H. Adams, 'Recent Developments in the Concept of Management in the Approved Schools', *Approved Schools Gazette*, 54:5, 1960, pp. 217–20.

[3] Gordon Rose, *Schools for Young Offenders*, London, Tavistock, 1967.

rary at times, that managers could be forgiven for not fully understanding the nature of their duties and tasks.

2 THE HOME OFFICE

The Home Office has been responsible for more innovations, improvements and changes, than any or all generations of managers and heads of schools. The changes which were imposed on the schools were partly based on spontaneous decisions within the Home Office (like the abolition of chains at Parkhurst), and partly derived from contemporary developments in the country as a whole, notably in medicine, psychology and sociology. But it has always been reluctant to spell out its powers and functions.

A recent Report has described the role of the Home Office as holding

the balance between the fostering of the independent life without which no school can work successfully, and the control necessary to secure that proper standards of accommodation, education and training are maintained, that accommodation is related to current needs, and that expenditure on the service is kept within proper limits.[1]

Sir Charles Cunningham, when he was Under-Secretary of State at the Home Office, described its functions in relation to Approved Schools under four headings:[2]

1 To keep policy under close and continuous review.
2 To organize the strategy of the schools in terms of types of schools and numbers of places required.
3 Day to day problems of administration and finance.
4 To give the schools cohesion and leadership.

These task descriptions do not make a clear distinction between aims and methods in Home Office function, which is our main interest. For this review, therefore, we will extract from these descriptions the three main stated functions: control, evaluation and leadership.

[1] Home Office, *6th Report on the Work of the Children's Department*, H.M.S.O., 1951, para. 240, p. 62.
[2] Sir Charles Cunningham in an address to the Conference of Approved School Heads, *Approved Schools Gazette*, 54:3, 1960, pp. 94–105.

Control

The theoretical and legally sanctioned powers of control held by the Home Office are very wide, but the available evidence suggests that there is a real reluctance to make use of them. Where control is exercised the approved school system may have become too complex for effective supervision from the centre.

The most pervasive control the Home Office exercises is in the field of finance where every detail of expenditure has to be approved both in estimate and in actual returns, yet there is no facet of administration which has been more severely criticized.[1]

Another indication of the unsatisfactory nature of the controlling function of the Home Office lies in the question of sanctions which they can impose on voluntary management committees. Unlike the paid employees in the inspectorate or amongst the staffs of approved schools, the Home Office had no real sanctions over managers except those applicable to the schools. In 1961 Parliament decided to provide a direct sanction which could be applied to managers. It gave powers to the Secretary of State to make orders regulating the constitution and proceedings of managers of any approved school (other than local authority schools) or to appoint additional managers.[2] The Home Office has made no use of these powers although they have now been in existence for six years[3] and at least one school has become the subject of an enquiry since then.[4] This reluctance to control in an effective way has also been referred to by Griffith.[5] A further difficulty is the curious position of the Home Office when trouble arises in a school which is sufficiently serious to warrant criminal proceedings. When this happens the Home Office will immediately withdraw inspections and withhold contact (i.e. control) in order, as they

---

[1] J. A. G. Griffith (*Central Departments and Local Authorities*, London, 1966, p. 419), mentions Public Accounts Committee Reports for 1956–1957, 1957–1958, 1962–1963, 1963–1964 as being severely critical. *The Eleventh Report of the Estimates Committee* (Session 1962–1963) stated quite bluntly that they were 'not satisfied that the financial control excerised by the Home Office is adequate'. H.M.S.O., 1963, 293, para. 30.

[2] Criminal Justice Act, 1961, Sect. 19(3).

[3] *Hansard*, 8 March 1967, Cols. 308–309.

[4] *Guardian*, 16 May 1967.   [5] Griffith, op. cit., p. 425.

say, to be able to go in when the situation has clarified, as an independent evaluating agent.[1] Another possible explanation for the apparent lack of effectiveness of control may lie in the organizational complexity of the whole system. This may be said to have two inevitable consequences which are related more to the nature of organizations than to the particular structure we are dealing with. In so large a system there are likely to be, in addition to formal goals, a number of subsidiary goals which will arise spontaneously among the various levels of social units within the organization. Thus, for example, although the official aims of the school may be the reformation, rehabilitation and social re-education of young offenders, as far as the boys are concerned their main goal may be to conform to the requirements of the school in order to secure an early release. The staff may comply with acceptable or unacceptable practices in order to ensure for themselves a reasonably satisfactory working situation and to enhance prospects of promotion.[2] Similarly, a headmaster may conform to Home Office and managerial control, even if he disagrees with it, in order to increase his reputation as an effective head and to ensure peace and security in his personal life. The managers, again, may conform to external control in order to gain a reputation for running an efficient school. The regional inspector may conform for the sake of promotion, and the headquarters inspectorate may conform for the sake of their reputation and to gain tolerant working conditions, and the administrators in the D1 section of the Home Office may adjust and conform in order to gain promotion within the Civil Service.[3] Achieving conformity may therefore be a much more realistic goal for all levels concerned with approved schools than the pursuit of ideals or the attempt to achieve complex and poorly-defined aims which are represented by such vague concepts as rehabilitation or social re-education.

This need for conformity is underlined by what might be

---

[1] P. Hornsby-Smith, 'Address to the Association of Managers', *Approved Schools Gazette*, 51:6, 1957, pp. 211–214.

[2] Charges of brutality against an approved school were made anonymously in the *Guardian* (2 March 1967) by a member of the staff who feared the loss of his house if he identified himself.

[3] D. Katz and R. L. Kahn, *Social Psychology of Organizations*, New York, John Wiley, 1965, p. 15.

described as possible self-contained conflict circuits which could be isolated in such a structure. At the purely theoretical level we might expect conflict between the administrators and the inspectorate, between the inspectorate and the regional inspectorate, between the inspectorate and the managers, between the headmasters and the staff, between the headmasters and the boys and between the staff and the boys.[1] The possibility of so many conflict areas would seem to make it both desirable and advisable for at least the majority of individuals involved to aim at a system of conformity which is not directed so much to specific aims and tasks, as towards creating a situation where life is tolerable and where conflict is reduced to a minimum. There is one line of evidence to suggest that this sort of argument is feasible. Most of those individuals who have strong views on the re-education of young offenders and who have made some attempt to introduce their ideas into the child-care system in this country have, so far as their ideas were non-conformist, had to remain outside the general system of the schools. People like A. S. Neill, G. A. Lyward, W. D. Wills and others, for all the general acceptance they now have in the field of social education, remain outside the approved schools system.[2] On the other hand, where new ideas are in strict conformity with the generally accepted standards of behaviour as prescribed by the Home Office there is no difficulty in introducing such ideas within the system itself. A good example is the experiment now being carried out at the Herts Training School under the supervision of the headmaster and a consultant psychiatrist.[3]

Evaluation

Historically there have been three main instruments of evaluation. The most valuable of these were the series of Commission and Committee Reports which provided periodic and syste-

[1] The likelihood of conflict is increased because these are nearly all boundary areas where role conflict is an additional hazard (see Katz and Kahn, op. cit., p. 192).

[2] See also Howard Jones, *Reluctant Rebels*, London, 1960, p. 9.

[3] D. Miller, 'A Model of an Institution for Treating Adolescent Delinquent Boys', in *Changing Concepts of Crime and its Treatment*, ed. H. Klare, London, 1966.

matic analyses of the entire system.[1] It is now forty years since the last of these enquiries was presented. All subsequent reports deal only with limited aspects of the system.[2] From the establishment of the Inspectorate in 1857 to 1911 the Home Office Inspectorate published annual reports which included a general survey of the school system and a brief report on every certified school. There was every opportunity, therefore, not only to follow the over-all developments in the system but also for the schools to compare their work and results with those of other schools. This could then be used as an invaluable guide to the relative importance, in failure and success, to be assigned to institutional policy and inmate characteristics. Between 1924 and 1963 only eight reports were published, one after a gap of ten years (1928–1938) and one after a gap of thirteen years (1938–1951). The Criminal Justice Act 1961 requires the Home Secretary to lay a report on approved schools, remand homes and attendance centres before Parliament every three years.[3] Apart from the irregularity and infrequency of Home Office Reports they have also changed considerably in content. Although some of the earliest reports were a little too outspoken and critical at the personal level,[4] they also contained closely-observed and carefully-analysed critical comments which in their totality represent an irreplaceable text on the nature and management of nineteenth-century institutions. Inasmuch as most of these comments are based on experience and observation, they still have a large measure of direct applicability today. Two examples may illustrate this:

Gradual change from influence to discipline is the chief disease of all large institutions; and reformatories depending for success so largely

[1] Especially those of 1884, 1896, 1913, 1927, which have already been referred to.

[2] Cf. the Durant and Ingleby Reports of 1960.

[3] The first of these was published in March 1964. See also Griffith, op. cit., p. 367. The inspectors' Reports are further discussed below, pp. 219–223 and 233–236.

[4] Cf. 'The superintendent is both trustworthy and well meaning and an excellent farm manager, but he has not sufficient ability or education for the post of superintendent.' *9th Report Inspector of Reformatory and Industrial Schools*, 1866, pp. 42–43. 'The mistress appears earnest and efficient but wanting in punctuality and order.' *First Report Inspector of Reformatory and Industrial Schools*, 1861, p. 61.

on the spirit that animates them and being liable to suffer so much when they grow too large for individual oversight, or pass from a superintendence of personal interest to one of professional routine . . . should be confined within moderate limits of numbers[1]. It cannot be kept too carefully in view by those who are entrusted with the management of reformatories that external order and methodical regulation cannot compensate for the want of sympathy and personal regard between themselves and the boys; and that the real spirit and proper results of a reformatory cannot be maintained unless the work of instruction, reproof and correction, which has to be carried out, is taken up as a chosen work of love and not merely discharged as an appointed duty.[2]

Since the Second World War, reports published by the Home Office have dealt with approved schools in the most general terms. No attempt is made at critical analysis and the purpose of the reports seems to be to reassure the public and support the staff and management rather than deal with precision and frankness with the problems and failures that are suggested by the available statistics.[3]

A third method of evaluation in which the Home Office was at first only marginally involved was the triennial meetings of managers and staffs of the schools. At these meetings those directly involved tried to conceptualize and give expression to what they were trying to achieve in the field. The records of these meetings are again very valuable not only for the prepared papers they reproduce but also for the free and frank discussions which always followed, which were faithfully recorded and which offer an excellent opportunity to study the climate of opinion on important issues among those most directly concerned. In recent years these meetings have come to be known as Home Office Conferences and have acquired a character of prestige meetings at which the Home Secretary or a high official of the Home Office will participate and which tend to rely increasingly on distinguished outsiders for ideas and information.[4]

---

[1] *Report Inspector of Reformatory and Industrial Schools*, 1861, p. 61.

[2] *Fourth Report*, op. cit., pp. 47–8.

[3] This also applies to the only publication from the Home Office designed to give the general public information about the schools. See *Making Citizens*, H.M.S.O., 1946.

[4] The Home Secretary of the day addressed the 1958 and 1964 Conferences. The Under-Secretary of State addressed the 1961 Conference. At

The results of these changes has been that hard, consistent, and valid information about approved schools is restricted to three uneven sources. The Home Office reports have already been referred to. A second source is rare publications like Gordon Rose's book,[1] while the third important source is the one so strongly deplored by all levels within the system, namely the reports of enquiries into riots and other irregularities and scandal items in books or newspapers.[2] One cannot resist the conclusion that the poor public image and public ignorance of approved schools is in some measure the result of the policy adopted by the Home Office, and perhaps by the schools themselves. One recent development may, however, alter this situation in time.

The Home Office Research Unit was established in 1957. It undertakes research into various aspects of criminology and penology, including studies related to approved schools. It also supports studies in universities and acts as a liaison and authorizing body for research workers.[3] It is not possible at this stage to say what influence the Unit will have in the long run or how and to what extent it will be able to influence the approved schools system. This may depend to some extent on the degree of professionalization within the approved schools system.[4]

---

these three conferences half the speakers were 'outsiders'. (*Approved Schools Gazette*, 52:5, 1958, 55:3, 1961, 58:8, 1964.)

[1] G. Rose, op. cit.

[2] The most recent 'scandal' followed the publication of a serious review of Rose's book in the *Guardian* (9 February 1967). Three recent novels have dealt with brutality in approved schools; *Teddy Boys Ahoy* by L. J. Harper, Dagenham, 1963; *The Division* by B. Meilen, London, 1967; and *Approved School Boy* by Stephen Slater, London.

[3] As at January 1967 there were thirteen research projects dealing in some way with approved schools (including this study). Of these, five were conducted by the Unit itself, two were conducted jointly by the Unit and school staffs, two were university projects financed by the Home Office, three were university projects approved by the Home Office, one is a project within an approved school. List of Current Research in Child Care, Adoption, Incidence and Prevention of Juvenile Delinquency, and Treatment of Young Offenders in England and Wales, Home Office Research Unit, Res. 636/4/11, January 1967, pp. 7–9.

[4] The writer's personal experience over a period of ten years suggests that there is a growing understanding of and interest in research in the Home Office. This is almost certainly due to the work of the Research Unit.

Leadership

In the final analysis, working with deprived, disturbed or delinquent children is an act of faith, a mission which will be demanding, baffling, exasperating and rewarding, no matter how much professional skill is devoted to it. All levels of staff engaged in this work need leadership and inspiration to sustain them and, as in the field of education, where leadership is lacking in the higher echelons of the structure, it is likely to be weak at the lower levels.[1]

Leadership implies the dissemination and affirmation of ideas and policies. In the residential-work field it is not nearly so important that such ideas should always be right but that they should be firmly and consistently expounded. Here again, as the historical analysis has shown, there has been a distinct change in the Home Office. Chief inspectors were once great names to all concerned with the schools, men of known character with strong convictions. Arthur Norris was the last of these and since he left the Home Office his successors have adopted the more typical Civil Service anonymity of the administrative branch of the Children's Department. Whether this is public policy or personal choice, it is clear that, while anonymity in no way suggests that recent chief inspectors are less able or competent than their predecessors, it has deprived them of the capacity for vigorous leadership, which certainly in periods of transition is essential. Because approved school work is so personal and so challenging it would seem unlikely that impersonally-conceived and impersonally-presented memoranda and circulars can take the place of personal leadership, nor can dynamic leadership be exercised by an administrative unit like the Children's Department.

This is why, originally, responsibility for the schools was given not to an office but to a person. The expansion of the administrative office has not eliminated the need for the individual leader. 'The Chief Inspector', Sir Edward Troup told the schools in 1911, 'should have the highest ideals for the schools – he should set these ideals before the schools, he should help the

---

[1] N. Gross and R. E. Herriot, *Staff Leadership in Public Schools*, New York, J. Wiley, 1965, especially Chapter 6.

schools to attain them and he should encourage, stimulate and co-operate with superintendents and managers in carrying out the highest ideals.'[1]

The inspectorate

From the passing of the first Reformatory School Act in 1854 until the appointment of Sydney Turner in 1857, certified schools were inspected by the prison inspectors of the area in which they were situated. Following the appointment of Turner a new department was set up to inspect reformatory (and later industrial) schools and to collect payment from parents. The inspector examined the schools two or three times a year and published an annual report in which he gave his findings in general terms and then described each school under the headings of premises, health, discipline, education, industrial training, staff, cost for the year, cost per head, and results on discharge. Associated with the inspector's office were agents in the main towns who collected payments from parents, but who also occasionally acted as advisers to the Courts.[2] The patterns of inspection were based largely on the immediate experience of the inspectors and the limitations of inspection as a method of control were soon recognized.[3] In 1881 Inglis outlined the limits of inspection:

The Government Inspection sees that the sanitary conditions of the buildings are what they should be and that the general appearance of the children on the date of inspection and the education state are satisfactory. It is the duty of the inspector to insist on practical industrial training; to point out deficiencies and to advise when he thinks that alterations in the buildings or management could be made with advantage; but as regards the treatment of the children

---

[1] *Certified Schools Gazette*, vol. 4:4, 1911, p. 68.

[2] Turner wrote of his agent in Glasgow that he had 'materially assisted the Magistrates in discriminating between the cases properly coming under the province and objects of the Industrial School Act and those which are subjects for charitable relief rather than detention at the cost of the Treasury'. *13th Report Inspector of Reformatory and Industrial Schools*, 1870, p. 28.

[3] There does not appear to have been an attempt to conceptualize the functions of inspection as was the case for inspectors in education. See N. Ball, *Her Majesty's Inspectorate 1839–1849*, Educational Monographs, University of Birmingham Institute of Education, 1963, Chapter 4.

during the year he has to depend to a great extent on the reports made to him by the superintendent and the book kept for his inspection and on information which comes to his ears from other quarters. More depends on the constant and careful supervision of a Committee, and when all has been done that can be done by the inspector and the committee of managers, it remains a fact that it is the master who makes the school and it is upon the appropriate selection of suitable masters that the success of the system to a great degree depends. No system of inspection, even a daily one, could ensure any school from outbursts of temper or occasional misconduct on the part of the superintendent but a good committee should be a safeguard against recurrences of such conduct and against systematic negligence and severity.[1]

The Royal Commission (1884) had no such misgivings about the scope of an inspector's function. They defined inspection as 'the machinery by means of which the Executive informs itself as to the condition of the Reformatory and Industrial Schools and their fitness to hold the official certificate and to receive the Treasury Grant'. But they did think that the inspector had too much work to do and suggested that his staff should be increased and that inspectors from the Board of Education should take over the inspection of education in the schools.[2] The Departmental Committee of 1896 was rather more critical and wanted some far-reaching changes. They thought that every school must be inspected three or four times a year because the inspector was 'the main outside influence that is brought to bear on these schools, exempt as they practically are from all intervention of parents'.[3] They saw the inspector as being a 'willing and encouraging adviser rather than a mere critic' but when the interests of the children demanded it he should be outspoken and firm and where necessary insist on dismissal of an inadequate superintendent. They also recommended the employment of a woman inspector for schools for girls and younger boys, and a part-time medical inspector particularly for nautical training ships. They were very critical about the reports published by the inspectors which they described as so vague that it was impossible to distinguish between good and bad schools from

[1] *25th Report Inspector of Reformatory and Industrial Schools*, 1882, pp. 10–11.
[2] *Report Royal Commission 1884*, op. cit., para. 18, p. 220.
[3] *Departmental Committee 1896*, op. cit., para. 197, p. 102.

them. They suggested a threefold purpose of the reports; to inform the government of the state of the schools, to show managers how their schools were doing, and to provide essential information for magistrates, school boards and police forces so that they would know what schools were appropriate for the children they were trying to place. The Committee recommended that future reports should be in two parts, one of which should be in the nature of a fairly static directory whilst the other would be a review of the schools in which failings and short-comings as well as good points were made explicit.[1] They concluded with a warning that 'for a long time to come – that is until higher standards have become more generally adopted – the influence of the central authority will have to be more actively exercised than has been the case in the past'.[2]

Inspections as such were not criticized by the Departmental Committee of 1913 but they wanted more of them because 'the fact that of recent years in certain cases serious evils have, owing to the insufficiency of inspectors, escaped notice is proof that more detailed and systematic investigation is necessary'.[3] They recommended that every school should be visited four times a year, that there should be a full-time medical inspector and that another woman inspector should be employed who was also to be medically qualified. They also suggested that vacancies in the inspectorate should be advertised to attract the most-highly qualified candidates. The Committee was extremely critical about the two-part annual reports which had been introduced following the recommendations of the Committee of 1896. They regarded these as 'practically useless', and thought that all that was really needed was a general report which dealt with items of public interest, while details about individual schools were to be exclusive to the Home Office and the respective managing committees.[4]

The schools themselves did not have a great deal to say about the function of the inspectorate, which most of them accepted absolutely, although there were individual protests when criticisms were felt to be unjust. Vine described inspections as very valuable to help schools to see themselves as others see them. He

[1] Ibid., p. 103. [2] Ibid., p. 104.
[3] *Departmental Committee 1913*, op. cit., p. 15.
[4] Ibid., p. 16.

thought criticisms made by the inspectors could be useful levers for getting buildings and staff changed when this was desirable.[1] He thought that boys enjoyed being inspected, although this is not borne out by Briggs who described inspections as

a confounded nuisance, being the cause of a prodigious amount of bustle, ill temper and a scrub-a-rub-dub for a week before. For two days we lived in our Sunday uniforms, hung listlessly about, were paraded and re-paraded and lived a distressing life. As far as I recollect [the inspector] never did any good and never any harm and certainly never discovered or saw anything he was not wanted to discover or see.[2]

In 1921 Norris had been Chief Inspector for four years, there had been no report since 1916 and individual reports of schools had ceased with the Departmental Committee of 1913. The *Certified Schools Gazette* published a strong protest because they felt neglected. The abolition of reports on individual schools

isolated each school from its neighbours for no one school could any longer get any idea of what others were doing. Further the Press which always commented on the publication, and selected interesting facts from the reports, were compelled to fasten on the exceptional circumstances that periodically arise in any and every system. . . . We urge upon Dr. Norris and urge very strongly, the desirability of reviewing the position with a view to the renewal of the older practice.

They complained that it had become 'the philosophy of modern inspection to find faults' but what they wanted to see was a fuller more comprehensive system of inspections which could broadly evaluate and publicize what the schools were trying to do.[3] Curiously enough, Norris appears to have been in agreement with the schools on the value of reports on individual schools: 'The schools have undoubtedly suffered from this lack of information as magistrates and social workers are apt to form their impressions only from the comparatively few cases of failure which come under their notice.' He reaffirmed that these reports were important to help managers and staffs of schools to review progress in their own schools in relation to others and to

[1] M. G. Vine, In *'Loco Parentis'*, London, 1905, pp. 67–8.
[2] I. Briggs, *Reformatory Reform*, London, 1924, pp. 85–6.
[3] *Certified Schools Gazette*, vol. 14:3, 1921, pp. 197–8.

keep the general public informed of what was happening.[1] Nevertheless, Norris did not reintroduce the old system and in fact discontinued the practice of even annual general reports.

Legally, the function of the inspectorate is only vaguely defined[2] and there is no published attempt by inspectors in recent years to conceptualize and define their roles, or to adapt them in the light of changing attitudes and increasing professionalization among staff. It would seem that the inspectorate still adheres very largely to the conception of its function outlined by Norris in his first report:

The aim of the inspectors is to help the schools by friendly constructive criticism and advice; to endeavour to secure progressive improvement by suggesting to schools methods which have been tried and proved successful in other schools; to watch over the administration of the large funds that are now made available for the support of the schools; and when the circumstances arise – though such incidents are becoming rarer each year – to protect children who from lack of oversight or ignorance show signs of unjust or harsh treatment.[3]

For all that, a strong case can be made for a fundamental reassessment of the role and functions of the inspectorate in relation to the approved schools as I suggested at the time of the Carlton School disturbance.[4] Schools today maintain standards in health, education, and general provisions which are probably better and more widely accepted than in many other countries, but so many complex and baffling problems of behaviour, disturbances and maladjustments are to be found in the population of the schools that one would have thought that questions of management and treatment should receive much more direct attention from the inspectorate, who are, after all, acting in an advisory capacity not only to the Home Office but also to the schools, than seems to be the case. Mechanical maintenance and physical standards in schools can be secured at a

---

[1] *First Report Children's Branch*, op. cit., 1923, p. 15.
[2] Children & Young Persons Act, 1933 (S. 103). See also Griffith, op. cit., p. 373.
[3] *First Report 1923*, op. cit., p. 54. This definition of function is very similar to one offered by Chief Inspector Scorrer in 1963. See *Eleventh Report – Estimates Committee*, H.M.S.O., 1963, pp. 95 and 106.
[4] J. Carlebach, *Brit. J. Crimin.*, vol. 1:2, 1960, pp. 197–200.

staff level lower than the inspectorate, who could then concentrate on the introduction of new methods of staff counselling and crisis intervention techniques which would be of much greater assistance to the schools, especially when such aids are offered with the support and authority of the central administration.[1]

Chief inspectors

Although the title of Chief Inspector was not used until Robertson was so designated in 1908,[2] there is a clear line of predecessors, and up to the appointment of the present chief inspector eight persons have held the post since it was first established in 1857.

Rev. Sydney Turner	1857–1876
Col. W. Inglis	1876–1896
J. G. Legge	1896–1906
T. D. M. Robertson	1906–1911
C. E. B. Russell	1913–1917
Dr. A. H. Norris	1917–1940
T. Paterson Owens	1940–1951
Miss A. M. Scorrer	1951–1965
Miss J. D. Cooper	1966

The most interesting and influential of these were Turner, Inglis, Legge, Russell and Norris.

Sydney Turner

When Turner was appointed Inspector he was one of the best-known figures in the reformatory school movement. He had successfully run England's first reformatory school for sixteen years and had taken a leading part in the agitation which led to the establishment of a nation-wide network of reformatories.

[1] An interesting experiment on these lines was carried out in Israel. See J. M. Rosenfeld and G. Caplan, 'Techniques of Staff Consultation in an Immigrant Children's Organization in Israel', *Americ. J. Orthopsych.* 24:1, 1954, pp. 46–62.

[2] M. A. Spielman, *The Romance of Child Reclamation*, London, Reformatory and Refuge Union, 1921, p. 120.

When he first took over the Philanthropic Society institution he established himself through his considerable capacity to learn from experience and his enormous intuitive understanding. These same characteristics were very marked when he became inspector. In his early reports there was a somewhat naïve assumption that the Act of 1854 would lead to the creation of institutions as effective and as carefully controlled as his own had been, but he soon realized that incompetence and mismanagement were much more likely than their opposites and for the best part of twenty years he vigorously pursued a policy of creating minimum standards, of reducing abuse and, more and more, as time went on, of trying to protect children in institutions from the worst effects of institutionalization. He commanded great respect from the schools, who recognized his profound knowledge of the field, but throughout his career remained reluctant to tackle those managers whose schools were not organized in the way they should have been. As a consequence he was unable to control many abuses, particularly in industrial schools, which were introduced by managers in an attempt to cope with their financial problems.

William Inglis

The next inspector is something of a mystery. He came from the Army, was unknown to the schools and although Turner's assistant, Henry Rogers, remained to serve under Inglis to give continuity,[1] Inglis was handicapped by not being able to speak with the forcefulness and authority that Turner could claim. In the classic tradition of the nineteenth-century ex-Army Civil Servant, Inglis applied himself to his task with absolute devotion and followed the approach of Turner so closely that it would be difficult to detect the change in inspectorate by merely reading the official reports. Unlike all the other inspectors Inglis rarely turned up in reports of social and professional meetings of reformatory school managers and superintendents. An additional handicap to his period of office was the rigidity which

[1] It is noteworthy that Rogers, in a review of reformatory school work in which he mentions every person of note in the movement, makes no mention of Inglis with whom he had worked for nearly twenty years. See *Reformatory and Industrial School Work*, seven lectures to the Reformatory and Refuge Union, London, 1898, esp. p. 132.

overtook so many institutions and for this Inglis was to some extent responsible, through his reluctance to commit himself, as for example, on the question of whether or not girls should go to prison before they went to a reformatory. This may well have caused the growing disinclination amongst managers to accept his strictures and recommendations. He tried desperately to eliminate the ill-treatment which children were subjected to in Truant Schools and pleaded in vain with institutions to reduce the amount of laundry work that girls had to do, and to abolish profitable but unhealthy employment for boys, like waste-paper sorting, match-making, wood-chopping and brick-making. In his last year of office Inglis was involved in a violent disagreement with the managers of a reformatory school ship. They refused to abide by his ruling and the issue was not resolved until the Home Secretary withdrew the school's certificate and as a result a new board of management was appointed.[1] Inglis left his post on this sad note and his disappearance was as mysterious as his arrival.

J. G. Legge

Legge came to the reformatory schools from the Prison Commission. The disagreement that ended Inglis's period of service and the Report of the Departmental Committee of 1896 probably seemed to Legge to be a clear justification for vigorous action to improve the whole school system. He liked to refer to the schools as Home Office Schools rather than Reformatories or Industrial Schools and almost threatened managers to comply with his demands or face the consequences.[2] His main interests lay in the field of health and education. He added to his normal duties the inspection of hearing and eyesight, constantly described the needs for and benefits of sports and exercises[3] and

---

[1] *39th Report – Inspector of Reformatory and Industrial Schools*, 1896, pp. 49–51.

[2] In his first report he warned that 'there will be no excuse in the future for the Reformatory which has not a good library', *39th Report* 1896, p. 36. In 1900 he wrote that 'if the present managers [of a school] are unable to maintain the ship in full efficiency, better hand her over to others', *43rd Report*, p. 160.

[3] 'The proper provision for genuine sports and games has a moral value of its own', *39th Report*, p. 39.

rejected out of hand the arguments put to Turner and Inglis that education ought to play only a secondary part in institutions for young offenders.[1] Legge attended and spoke at every meeting that dealt with his schools, wrote pamphlets on the schools both for this country and for America and established in the Reformatory and Refuge Union the Legge Library which for many years must have been the best and most comprehensive criminological library in this country outside the British Museum.[2] Legge left the Home Office when he was still comparatively young to become Director of Education in Liverpool, and one is bound to wonder whether his premature departure from the Home Office was not due to his perhaps too volatile approach to the influential but somewhat conservative managers of the schools.

C. E. B. Russell

Russell died after only four years at the Home Office. In spite of this he is one of the best-remembered inspectors and the Home Office and the schools arrange an annual lecture by some distinguished person in his memory.[3] Russell was a youth club worker in Manchester where he took a keen interest in the problems of delinquency. He published an excellent book on the subject in 1906[4] and probably as a result of this was invited to

[1] 'I have heard two propositions put forward . . . a) that to educate the inmates of reformatories beyond the 5th standard will do no moral good, b) that it will do moral harm. The truth of the former proposition I doubt, the truth of the latter I absolutely deny.' Ibid., p. 36.

[2] Money for the library was originally subscribed by managers and staff of the schools when Legge resigned (£183) though it seems that his leaving was regretted more by the staffs than by the managers of the schools. See *Seeking and Saving*, vol. xxi, 1906, pp. 194–201. The library was opened in 1908.

[3] Charles Russell Memorial Lectures were established by a bequest of his widow in 1948 and have been held annually since 1952. The head of the Home Office Children's Department and the Secretary of the National Association of Boys Clubs are the trustees. See *7th Report on the work of the Children's Department*, H.M.S.O., 1955, p. 48, and *Charles E. B. Russell, A Memoir*, re-published by the trustees in 1958.

[4] C. E. B. Russell and L. M. Rigby (later Mrs. Russell), *The Making of the Criminal*, London, 1906. He also published other books, *Working Lads' Clubs* (1908) and *Young Gaol Birds* (1910).

become a member of the Departmental Committee which was appointed in 1911 and which reported in 1913, the year that Russell was appointed Chief Inspector. Russell was a man full of ideas and these he set out gently but determinedly in the few reports published under his name. His ideas were to some extent revolutionary[1] and were often resisted by managers and staff but he was so gentle in his approach, so determined in his attitudes and so enthusiastic about the good effects that the changes he was advocating would have, that he managed to carry many schools with him, sometimes perhaps against their better judgement.

A. H. Norris

Norris was a medical inspector serving under Russell. During the war years he was on active service until his appointment to the chief inspectorate in 1917.[2] Norris was the man who made the schools what they are today and who probably exercised a greater influence over the Children's Department of the Home Office than any other person hitherto, but his long and fruitful period of office has not been fully described and analysed. One of the first things that Norris did was to put the schools on a sound financial footing by creating the system which is used to this day, of the Home Office paying half the cost of the schools and the local authorities paying the other half. He shared responsibility for everything he did with the Assistant Under-Secretary of State in charge of the Children's Department. There is some indication that at any rate during his first years of office Norris had a basic dislike of institutions.[3] It has already

[1] He firmly advocated consulting parents about their children, replacing enamel crockery with chinaware in institutions and abolishing the rule that children must eat their meals in silence. His favourite tool for reformation was the cultivation of self-respect.

[2] Norris was a disciple of Russell. He had been associated with him since 1901 in social and boys' brigade work in Manchester. Norris had a wide experience of children through his medical and social work in the slums and schools of Manchester (see *Certified Schools Gazette*, vol. 10:4, 1917, p. 316).

[3] His first major address to the Reformatory and Refuge Union in May 1918 (i.e. about six months after his appointment) was entitled 'The Limitations of Institutional Training' in which he described the ideal for the child in need, the effort to make his 'home fit for the child and give the child

been shown that during the 1920s the schools were at their lowest point in public esteem and at their most effective and successful in terms of the work they were doing. Norris made good use of this situation to try to lever the schools into those attitudes and approaches which he regarded as desirable. He published his first report in 1923, expressing regret that he was as yet unable to resume the old practice of reviewing every school but promising to do so in the future.[1] Although annual reports were published in 1924 and 1925 he made no attempt to revert to the old practice of using the reports to compare and review the schools. Instead, his inspectorate was incorporated into the Children's Department,[2] and the reformatory and industrial schools became just one aspect of the wide and varied functions of that Department.[3] In 1928 Norris published another report in which he explained that he had come to the conclusion that it would be better to publish occasional reports on problems of delinquency and child neglect rather than annual reports dealing with schools that catered for only a small section of the classes of children he was interested in. Norris is said to have been the main architect of the Children and Young Persons Act of 1933.[4] In addition to his report he published many papers on various aspects of child-care and institutional management.[5] He can clearly claim the distinction of having served longest in his post, of having been most influential, of introducing the greatest changes in the approved school system, including the change of nomenclature, and of being the last of

---

sufficient strength of character to return to its home, even if it is not all tha can be desired'. *Seeking and Saving*, 1918, vol. xx, pp. 48–54. In April 1919 he produced a report on the schools in which he was exceptionally critical of them. See below pp. 89–90.

[1] *Home Office – First Report on the Works of the Children's Branch*, 1923, p. 15.

[2] *Home Office – 2nd Report on the Work of the Children's Branch*, H.M.S.O., 1924, p. 2.

[3] These now included juvenile courts, probation, the employment and protection of children, etc.

[4] Personal communication from Mr. John Gittins, principal of the Aycliffe Classifying Approved School who joined the Children's Branch of the Home Office in 1936 and worked with Norris.

[5] His last paper, 'Nocturnal Enuresis in Institutions for Children' was published in 1943 (see *Approved Schools Gazette*, vol. 36:7, 1943, pp. 194–198).

the great chief inspectors to control the schools by open and forceful leadership.[1]

The reports of the chief inspectors deserve much greater attention than they have received. They are riddled with comments and observations which are very often gems of succinct and insightful expressions of the needs and problems of staff and children in institutions. It is interesting to note the differing techniques adopted by the leading figures in the inspectorate. Both Turner and Inglis used what one might call the comparison and common-sense approach. They went from school to school, observed what went on, assessed it by their own standards of right and wrong, compared its effectiveness with practices in other institutions and then laid down clearly-argued rules as to what should and what should not be done. They implicitly accepted the rights of managers and superintendents to experiment, to be different, and even, at times, to do what seemed to them not altogether desirable if those who did it could make a good case for it and above all could show that it worked.[2] Legge on the other hand rushed into the schools with many excellent but preconceived notions and tried to force the changes he wanted. Russell was not unlike Legge in his approach but he preferred gentle persuasion to forceful demands. He painted rosy pictures for the schools of the wonderful things to be expected if they would only follow his advice and adopt his ideas. Norris used yet another approach. He consistently and repeatedly referred to the things he disliked most and the things he was most determined to change by either describing them as deplorable occurrences in one or two schools or, more often, by describing them as deplorable occurrences of the past. Although Norris's system clearly worked it has had the unfortunate consequence that a great deal of valuable,

[1] Significantly, Norris was also the last chief inspector to publish signed reports.

[2] E.g. 'The boys are a little rough in manner, but this arises rather from the thoroughly plain farm house style of their training than from any want of control or discipline.' *4th Report Inspector of Reformatory and Industrial Schools*, 1861, p. 32. 'A good many cases of absconding. This results in a great measure from the system pursued by Mr. Atty of placing the boys out on licence to employment at an early age. Some independence and restlessness is set up but the final result is not discouraging.' *17th Report Inspector of Reformatory and Industrial Schools*, 1874, p. 55.

constructive, and progressive work in residential child-care which was carried out and recorded between 1854 and 1920 was, and has remained, rejected, partly because for more than twenty years Norris made a habit of saying that that which was past was bad.

3 ADMINISTRATION OF THE SYSTEM TODAY

Central government

All approved schools are directly controlled by the Children's Department of the Home Office.[1] This department is subdivided into three divisions and an inspectorate. One of the divisions deals with approved schools and remand homes, and some inspectors specialize in problems of approved schools. The other two divisions have marginal interests in approved schools. D2 counts as one of its functions the study of juvenile delinquency, and D3 specializes in questions of training, which include the training of staff for approved schools. The divisions are staffed by administrators who are not necessarily specialists in the fields they deal with. Inspectors act as professional advisers to the administrative staff and have no decision-making powers.

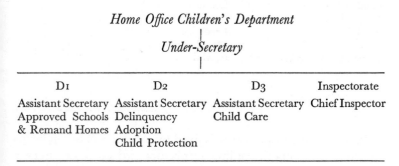

Home Office Children's Department			
Under-Secretary			
D1	D2	D3	Inspectorate
Assistant Secretary	Assistant Secretary	Assistant Secretary	Chief Inspector
Approved Schools & Remand Homes	Delinquency Adoption Child Protection	Child Care	

The inspectorate has a headquarters section in London consisting of:

[1] J. A. G. Griffith, *Central Departments and Local Authorities*, London, Allen & Unwin (for Royal Institute of Public Administration), 1966, esp. pp. 359–428.

1 Chief Inspector
2 Deputy Chief Inspectors (including one who specializes in approved schools)
1 Senior Medical Inspector
12 Specialist Inspectors (Training – Care of Children under five – Dietetics – Preventive Work – Approved School Work)
4 Medical Inspectors
1 Part-time consultant Psychiatrist.

The main body of the inspectorate is divided into seven regions in England and Wales. Each region is controlled by a superintending inspector.

TABLE 3
Regional inspectorate
(January 1965)

Region	Based on	Number of Inspectors (including Superintending Inspectors)
London North	London	11
London Central	London	9
London South	London	10
Midlands	Birmingham	8
North East	Leeds	10
North West	Manchester	9
Wales and South West	Cardiff	8
	Total	65

Policy for the inspectorate is fixed by meetings between headquarters and superintending inspectors two or three times a year. The entire inspectorate meets every two or three years.

Communication between the Home Office and the approved schools system as a whole is through the Approved Schools Central Advisory Committee which includes representatives from the Home Office, the Associations of Managers and Approved Schools Heads, and Staff Associations.

Approved schools are visited on average three times a year. Visits usually last about two hours and are generally but not always announced in advance. During his visit the inspector will check the school records, talk to staff and children and note the general atmosphere of the school. He may also join in a meal. These periodic visits are followed up by discussions when the inspector will comment on his findings. Subsequently an informal letter is sent. A written report on the visit is submitted to the headquarters inspectorate in London though, as Griffiths[1] has noted, while inspectors are very outspoken in their reports, they are 'much less direct' in their discussions with schools. Apart from periodic visits, special visits may be made with specific objects in mind, e.g. investigating complaints. Once every seven years every school undergoes a 'full inspection' when headquarters and regional inspectors combine to examine every facet of school life separately.[2] Thus, each inspector takes on one aspect of the school, e.g.,

Premises and equipment
Management
Staff
Daily routine
Vocational training
Parental contacts
Fire precautions.

Although inspectorial supervision is thus fairly comprehensive, direct contact between D1 and the Managers, and D1 and the headmasters also exists.

The *Handbook*[3] has described Home Office responsibilities in detail. These include reviewing the school population in relation to the number of places available and the number of committals requiring places, the increase or decrease of accommodation in individual schools and where necessary the provision of new places, the classification of schools according to the type of child they will admit, the determination of the maximum number a school is capable of handling (the so-called

[1] Griffith, op. cit., p. 425.
[2] Addendum, *The Gibbens Report* (Cmnd. 3367), 1967, states that owing to pressure of work these periodic visits do not now take place (p. 7).
[3] *Handbook for Managers*, op. cit.

certified numbers), the whole range of correspondence and memoranda in relation to the schools, the inspection of schools and contact with committees of management as required. Detailed powers exist in relation to each school. The Home Office has the right to examine minutes of meetings and all log-books kept by management committees and headmasters. They have complete financial control over estimates and actual expenditure and authorize all expenditures by the schools. They authorize additions and alterations to premises, approve the appointment of headmasters and also have a selection board for those members of staff below the rank of headmaster who do not have formal qualifications and who must be approved by this board before they can be employed. The Home Office approves daily routines, schemes of education and training, awards and privileges and pocket-money scales for individual schools, and has the power to authorize transfer of individual boys and girls from one school to another.

The managers

Although the managers of approved schools are generally regarded as an entity, they should properly be divided into three separate groups on the basis of their distinctive administrative structures. Of 119 schools,[1] 60 were managed by local (ad hoc) committees, 29 were managed by voluntary or religious societies, and 30 were managed by local authorities. The special features of these groups can best be described under these headings.

Local (ad hoc) committees

These committees represent the original form of management and 26 of the 60 schools in this group were founded in the nineteenth century. They include the four classifying schools and reflect the incidence of delinquency fairly accurately in the distribution of types of schools.

[1] When this enquiry began there were 121 schools but two girls' schools were closed between March and May 1966.

Local committees

Classifying boys	4
Senior boys	17
Intermediate boys	12
Junior boys	10
Senior girls	8
Intermediate girls	5
Junior girls	4
	60

Managing committees elect themselves and many of them still reflect the upper-class image of their Victorian origins. Because local authorities pay half their costs, they now often co-opt a member of their authorities and in many instances have deliberately tried to enrol professional people, particularly from universities in their areas. Inevitably, they tend to include the best and the worst committees and the most subservient and difficult relations with the Home Office. Their independence may act as a stimulus to experiment but equally it may and does increase their sense of confusion and perplexity when there is no influence amongst them to channel and interpret the changes which are constantly being imposed.

Voluntary or religious societies

The 29 schools in this group are usually classed together with Local Committee Schools, as voluntary committees, but the administrative structure of the two groups makes it necessary to treat them separately. The distribution of types of schools in this group reflects the predominant concerns of the societies in Victorian times.

Voluntary/religious societies

Senior boys	3
Intermediate boys	6
Junior boys	8
Senior girls	7
Intermediate girls	3
Junior girls	2
	29

The important feature of this group is the differentiation between main committees responsible for the policy of the society, and the local or house committee responsible for a single institution. The general trend in these societies appears to follow a model laid down in the 1930s. According to this model, nearly all major decisions are made at headquarters in line not only with Home Office direction but also with society policy, whilst the house committee deals with the minutiae of day-to-day administration. The societies generally appoint members to house committees, sometimes at the suggestion of local members. Appointment of senior staff, questions of finance and change, remain with the society. House committees concern themselves with the health, education and leisure activities of inmates and act in a supervisory capacity to the headmaster or matron. Main committees often send one of their members to sit with house committees to represent the society's interests.[1] Our survey suggests that this basic pattern has not changed very much and that there is considerable frustration in being subjected to this dual control by the society and the Home Office.

Local authority schools

Thirty approved schools are managed by local authorities, but these are unevenly distributed over the range of schools in that they cater mainly for boys of school age, again reflecting a historical trend. Local authorities came into this work originally through industrial schools.

Local authority schools

Senior boys	6
Intermediate boys	8
Junior boys	12
Senior girls	4
	—
	30
	—

[1] 'The Functions of a House Committee', *Seeking and Saving*, vol. xxxiv, 1934, pp. 66–7.

The managers of these schools are drawn from the Children's Committee of the respective authorities, including the children's officer, who is a paid professional person. Although the managers are thus mainly elected councillors, eight of the twenty-four authorities who manage schools co-opt private individuals with special experience of the field on to their committees, though there is a marked difference between county and city councils regarding this practice.

TABLE 4

*Co-optation of private persons on local authority
managing committees*[1]

Type of authority	No.	Co-opt	Do not co-opt
County councils	12	10	2*
City & borough councils	12	6	6†
	24	16	8

* One of these co-opts councillors from neighbouring authorities.

† One of these has co-opted former councillors with experience of this committee but would not co-opt private individuals. One used to have private members who have not been replaced following their death or retirement.

The most important feature of local authority management is its professional framework. Whatever the degree of amateurism of the managers, their deliberations are based on professional guidance from specialists in child care, finance, maintenance of buildings, health and education. In view of the extensive control from the Home Office one would anticipate a greater degree of co-operation and mutual understanding, if only because the local authority administrators are themselves civil servants with methods of planning and communication most like those used in central government. For the same reasons, however, conflict and a sense of frustration may be more intense. Detailed guidance, which may be meaningful when directed to people with more goodwill than skill, could be

[1] This table is based on information provided by the twenty-four local authorities.

very irritating to experienced workers. Again, whilst the *ad hoc* committee manager derives his authority from the Home Office, the local authority manager may feel that he comes into such a committee armed with the authority of a mandate from the electorate. Some of these irritations have been recorded by Griffith who found that local authorities were not too keen to take on approved schools because of the stringent financial control exercised by the Home Office and because the Home Office was 'always breathing down your neck'.[1]

ORGANIZATIONAL STRUCTURE OF APPROVED SCHOOLS

Main decision-making units on the left of each column, advisory on the right.

Local committee schools	Voluntary society schools	Local authority schools
Home Office	Home Office	Home Office
H.Q. inspectorate	H.Q. inspectorate	H.Q. inspectorate
Regional inspectors	Regional inspectors	Regional inspectors
	H.Q. committee	Managers
Managers	Soc. admin staff	L. A. professional staff
	Local committee	
Headmaster	Headmaster	Headmaster

OTHER STAFF
|
BOYS AND GIRLS

Heads of approved schools

These form the third pillar in the administrative structure of the schools. As will be seen from the analysis of duties, in a formal context the head is mainly responsible for the orderly, disciplined function of the school. He is also the link between boys and managers, staff and managers, and inspectorate and managers. His true role and function are, however, much more complex and diffuse than his formal duties would suggest. His task is sufficiently unique to warrant a separate investigation which is, however, beyond the scope of this study.

[1] Griffith, op. cit., p. 409.

The duties and functions of management[1]

The duties and functions of approved school managers are wide-ranging, complex and extensive. They are based on codified rules and are remarkable in that they combine vague, open instructions (e.g. maintain efficient standards) and precise, petty details (e.g. get advice from local fire officer).

There are six main areas of responsibility.

1 Managing committees
2 Finance
3 Building and maintenance
4 Staff
5 Children
   (a) Legal
   (b) Health and welfare
   (c) Training and discipline
   (d) Release and supervision
   (e) Parents
6 Home Office and inspectorate

In order to underline the extent of managerial responsibility in relation to the Home Office and heads of schools, the formal duties of all three levels of authority have been summarized.

Managing committees

Managers are expected to have suitable knowledge and experience for their task. Every committee is required to have a chairman and correspondent (secretary) and a treasurer. It is obligatory for managers to form release and finance sub-committees, but training, welfare, maintenance and education sub-committees are optional. The full committee should meet once a month and at least one manager must visit the school monthly. It is expected, however, that managers, a proportion of whom must live within reasonable distance of the school, will pay frequent visits, will visit at various times of day without prior notice and will ensure that they know, and are known by, the

[1] This summary is based on the *Approved School Rules*, 1933, as amended in 1949, and the *Handbook for Managers*, 1961 (circulated privately by the Home Office).

school. Full minutes of committee and sub-committee meetings must be kept as well as log-books of visits and a release register. The headmaster and the medical officer should attend meetings to report on their activities. It is the duty of the Board of Management to make the work of their school known both to the general public and to the local community in which they are situated. They must also notify the Home Office of any changes in management.

The Home Office has the power to appoint at least one member to the committee and inspect all minutes of meetings, log-books and registers.

The headmaster should act as a link between the managers and the school.

Finance

Managers must submit estimates of expenditure for the year in a preliminary and revised estimate. At the end of the financial year a summary of income and expenditure must be submitted to the Home Office. Special approval has to be obtained for any additional or unforeseen expenditure as well as for compensation to be paid from school accounts. Maintenance bills for individual children must be submitted to the local authorities. Schools having private funds need not seek approval for using these but must submit them to audit. Money belonging to boys remains subject to their own wishes. Special approval has to be sought for providing dental equipment. Accounts of local authority schools are audited by the district auditor, for voluntary schools by a private local chartered accountant. The Home Office must be informed of any change of auditor.

The Home Office has full control over estimates. It receives financial reports from managers, guides their expenditure and sends authority for expenditure to be incurred. It fixes fees for auditors and communicates directly with private accountants engaged by the schools.

The headmaster may only incur petty expenditure.

Building and maintenance

Managers must maintain efficient standards in the condition of the school. They must arrange for routine maintenance to be carried out, inspect the school log-book regularly and insure the school and its contents. They must get advice from the local fire officer and test the effectiveness of fire practice. They must ensure proper standards for the safety of all machinery and maintain a register of outside employments. They must seek Home Office approval for any substantial additions, demolitions or alterations of buildings and use Home Office architects.

The Home Office authorizes additions to and alterations of premises.

Staff

Managers appoint, suspend and dismiss staff. In voluntary schools all appointments and terminations of staff must be notified to the Home Office who should be consulted on all appointments. Home Office approval should also be obtained for engaging paid local help. Managers must appoint suitable after-care agents. They must maintain a proper balance between young and experienced staff, they should ensure female influence in boys' schools and provide good accommodation for staff. They must approve of the way the headmaster disposes of his staff, encourage staff to undertake training, seek Home Office approval for engaging temporary staff while regular staff undergo training and for all extraneous duties. They must ensure that competent staff are employed for adventurous activities, approve the absence of the headmaster for more than two days, appoint medical and dental officers and hear staff grievances after the headmaster.

The Home Office approves the appointment of all heads of schools and approves unqualified staff for employment after appearance before a selection board.

The headmaster determines the duties of the staff, is the first in line to receive staff grievances and must seek approval from managers and inform the chief inspector if he is absent from the school for two or more days.

Children

(a) Legal: Managers have the legal rights and powers of parents. In cases of violent or sudden death they must notify the coroner. They cannot legally refuse to accept an absconder and they must obtain insurance cover for all adventurous activities.

The Home Office authorizes charges brought against absconders.

The headmaster must send any inquest proceedings in cases of violent or sudden death, to the chief inspector.

(b) Health and welfare: The managers must maintain efficient health and welfare standards, and must ensure proper provisions for both. They must be present at least monthly when meals are served and see that boys know that they have a right of access to the managers. They must protect boys from unsettling visitors and have the power to send boys to hospital.

The Home Office approves the daily routines of the school.

The headmaster must ensure the health of the boys. In cases of death from illness or accident he must notify the parent or guardian and the chief inspector.

(c) Training and discipline: Managers must maintain efficient standards of training and education. They must make appropriate arrangements for religious instructions and know the school marks system, decide with the head on any action to be taken if boys cause loss or damage and approve requests for transfer to the Home Office. They must see that home leave is not lightly withheld and must give written consent for the detention of boys for more than twenty-four hours. They must also give special approval for boys over fifteen to receive twelve strokes of the cane. Managers may authorize principal teachers to give up to two strokes of the cane on the hand to boys under fifteen. They must examine punishment books which the chairman must sign, and submit this quarterly to the medical officer. Managers must report details of all irregular punishment to the Home Office and decide whether such irregular punishments require further action.

The Home Office approves schemes of education and training and of awards and privileges. It authorizes the transfer of boys between schools.

The headmaster is responsible for the efficient conduct of the school. He must maintain a good tone in the school and maintain discipline. He must keep records of pocket money that is withheld and of serious punishments. He must examine the punishment book kept in the school-room and must also record all irregular punishments.

(d) Release and supervision: Managers must continue to care for boys on supervision. They have statutory responsibilities to place a boy out on supervision as soon as is justified, to consider a release date at regular review meetings, to keep a release register and to receive written reports on every boy at least every term. In assessing a boy's suitability for release the following criteria are to be used: general behaviour, suitability, response to education and training, progress in relation to reason for committal, prospects of employment, the desirability of returning the boy to his home and any need for special placements. Managers must provide a leaving outfit and money for travel and subsistence. They should arrange for the boy to be visited, help him with suitable employment and lodging or a hostel if needed. They must revoke the supervision and recall the boy if this is deemed necessary. The revocation and recall must be in writing. During the period of supervision managers retain parental rights except when the boy lives with his parents.

(e) Parents: The headmaster must inform the boy's parent or guardian of the child's arrival at the school. Managers must make adequate provision for parental visits and obtain parental consent for all adventurous activities.

Home Office and inspectorate

Managers should discuss their plans with the superintending inspector and consult regularly with visiting inspectors. They should invite an inspector to attend one of their meetings once a year.

The Home Office review school populations in relation to places and committals, and increase or decrease accommodation, including the provision of new places, according to demand. It classifies schools and fixes the maximum number of boys any school may receive (certified numbers). It contacts all official correspondents and issues memoranda relating to the work of the schools. It inspects all schools, and inspectors meet managers as needed.

The headmaster must advise managers when the inspector arrives.

Management in practice

The following list of duties for managers of one Approved School will illustrate how this administrative complex can be translated into practice.

Mr. A   Trustee manager
Licensing in 'X' house
House organization
The chaplain and religious instruction
Contact with the inspectorate
Contact with the school medical and dental officers
Contact with the school psychiatrist.

Mr. B   Licensing in 'Y' house
Finance
Office administration
The Bursar in so far as these matters affect his work.

Mr. C   Trustee manager
The farm
The farm manager and his staff
The gardener and the garden

Mr. D   Trustee manager
Licensing in 'Y' house
Maintenance and improvement in buildings
Staff houses
Estate management matters
The Bursar in so far as these matters affect his work.

Mr. E   Licensing in 'Z' house
Catering, i.e. Special dietary scale
Catering, i.e. Control of Purchase
Catering, i.e. Departmental transfer systems
The Catering Officer

Evening Clubs
Building and Allied Trades Council Meetings.

Mrs. F   Licensing in 'Z' house
Catering
The female staff

Mrs. G   Licensing in 'Y' house
The female staff.

Mrs. H   Licensing in 'X' house
The female staff
The principal teacher and the school-room.

Mr. J   Licensing in 'Y' house
Organized athletic activities and sports
Adventurous activities – camping, youth hostel-
ling, swimming
Duke of Edinburgh Award Scheme
The instructors and the workshops
Scheme of awards and privileges
Pocket money
Incoming and outgoing mail.

Mr. K   Licensing in 'Z' house
The instructors and the workshops
Schemes of practical training
Employment on work outside the school.

Mr. L   Trustee Manager
Licensing in 'Y' house
Scouts, cadets
Adventurous activities, Duke of Edinburgh
Award Scheme
Staff salaries, agreements, retirement, liaison,
training.

It should be noted, however, that this division of duties comes from a school which has devoted some time to devising a workable scheme. Not all schools have done this, especially in cases where managers are involved with more than one school.

4 APPROVED SCHOOL MANAGERS[1]

In May 1966 there were 1,508 manager *places* for 119 approved schools. 952 of these were held by men and 556 by women. Manager places are specified because the actual number of managers is rather less owing to a certain amount of multiple representation, especially in local authority schools, where one manager may sit on the boards of from two to six schools.

In boys' schools the distribution of men to women managers is about three to one, while in girls' schools there are about two women to every man manager. Most managers (men and women) are well beyond middle age and quite a number are retired. About half the managers have served their schools for from ten to thirty-five years. Those managing independent schools tend to have the longest records of service. Again about half the managers are university or professionally trained and managers tend to hold or to have held predominantly 'middle class' occupations. There are fewer professionals on local authority committees but there is no evidence that professionals as managers differ markedly from non-professionals in their attitudes to approved-school work.

Managers engage in this form of voluntary social work mainly because they are interested in the welfare of young people and in their local community affairs. They are much less likely to become involved, because as, say, professionals they have a specific contribution to make arising from their main occupation.

Even so, quite a few managers are concerned with various aspects of child welfare and delinquency apart from approved-school management. Women who become managers are often also involved in other public affairs.

Most managers meet once a month in full committee. This is a statutory requirement but most of the work is done in various sub-committees which may meet as frequently as once a week. Apart from formal meetings, however, there are many managers who do not visit their schools often enough, especially among

[1] This section is a summarized version of a survey of managers carried out in 1966. See Julius Carlebach, 'Authority and Responsibility in Reformatory and Approved School Management', unpublished M.Litt. thesis, University of Cambridge, 1968.

local authority managers. They tend to have little contact with youngsters who have been released from the schools.

Unlike their Victorian ancestors, managers today make little attempt to act as links between the schools and their local communities. In spite of the heated debate surrounding the schools, managers are, on the whole, satisfied with the basic principles of approved-school training, though there are sharply divergent opinions amongst them. Few managers see themselves nowadays as assuming the roles of the parents of the youngsters in the schools, though legally that is their position (*in loco parentis*). Many managers would welcome greater public support for their work but they tend to be a little ambivalent in their attitudes to research, which most of them would welcome provided it was not in their schools.

There is a great deal of confusion and uncertainty about the role and functions of managers and in the following pages some of the views expressed by managers about various aspects of their work are presented.

Aspects of Management

Function

There were clear views on what the function of managers was –

Managers should deal with disputes, crises and conflict situations. They should inform themselves on what is being done through reports, visits, etc., but interfere as little as possible.

But there was also doubt –

I am extremely confused about duties of managers and how much time they ought to take up.

The voluntary principle

Some managers thought that the voluntary system was very good –

The managers are usually not involved with the local councils and therefore do not bring politics into their work. I think that the voluntary managers' system of government is the most satisfactory.

Others saw disadvantages –

All managers at my school are voluntary amateurs. Perhaps some assistance from an experienced and qualified professional is needed.

Decision making

One manager was sure of his powers –

Managers of approved schools really do take decisions of importance.

But others were not so sure –

By the time matters of importance reach the managers' meeting, decisions have already been made and the managers are required to 'rubber stamp' them.

Local authority managers

Unlike other managers, those from local authorities are appointed automatically or politically –

As chairman of the children's committee I am automatically manager.

Managers in general are appointed owing to their affiliation with political parties.

Objections to this system are based partly on time-consuming commitments elsewhere, and partly on lack of understanding of children's problems –

In my opinion the recruitment of managers arbitrarily from the local council members is almost wholly bad . . . too many local committees are created by a process of purely political proportional representation and while this is acceptable for dealing with sewage disposal, it is a most unacceptable method of dealing with children.

Voluntary managers were seen to have definite advantages –

I think that voluntarily managed schools attract people as managers who are able to devote more time and interest to character building.

Administratively there were two points of view. On the one hand the ability to call on professional staffs was regarded as an asset –

The administration from the angle of finance, architects for planning etc., and the local aspects are all taken care of by the various departments of the council as well as over-all care of the boys and staff by the children's officer of that department.

and comparison was made with voluntary managers who lacked direct experience of general problems of child care. On the other hand, administrative duplications were seen as a handicap, and the 'liberality' of the authority could become an issue.

Voluntary society managers

One society has listed the qualities it looks for in managers; but some of those selected felt less sanguine –

It is sometimes difficult to assess the real responsibility of the managers when the school is run by a voluntary [religious] organization for the Home Office.

Training for managers

Some managers felt that training and more conferences might be helpful –

I think that the time has passed when the pure amateur is of value as an approved school manager. All managers should have training and/or professional experience in dealing with children.

All managers have a great deal to learn about approved schools.

The conferences that take place are excellent but are very few and far between. As the chairman very rightly wishes to attend and as there are normally only two invitations, the rest of us do fare rather badly.

Professionals as managers

Professionals who are co-opted on to managing committees are not necessarily fully effective or happy in their positions –

When I was first appointed a manager of an approved school I was full of enthusiasm and attended very regularly. After realizing that all that was required of me was to listen to the monthly report and approve of all that was said and done and that my views (as a social worker) were contrary to the established ones and very far from welcome, I have withdrawn to a large extent.

Managers' views on managers

There was criticism of other managers; some of which concerned their attitudes –

I have felt certain ambivalence amongst my fellow managers at times. They are uncertain whether to treat or punish.

Despite the fact that I am sure my fellow managers wish to do good, they have the failing of seeing the need to protect society rather than seeing the 'needs of the children'.

and some the length of time managers tend to remain –

It might stimulate the work if managers instead of being appointed in perpetuity were re-elected at, say, seven-year intervals.

There was concern about the lack of young recruits –

I feel very strongly that managers ought to be ideally very much younger than those I have come across.

about local representation –

I am constantly convinced that more local representation of managers is vital to approved schools. At my school I am the only local, the other managers coming from very far afield and visits more or less are confined to official meetings.

about time factors limiting selection –

The need to find time during the working day clearly limits the choice of managers.

Visiting the schools

On visits to schools and committee meetings there were mainly descriptive comments and suggestions.

Contacts with boys and girls

Where contact with boys and girls was commented upon, there was some satisfaction –

My school has a system of 'families', each manager being allocated 10–12 boys. I visit mine at least once per month and have a private chat with each of them.

but rather more dissatisfaction –

I have had no close personal contact with the girls in the school as my time has been largely occupied in my work as treasurer.

Home Office and Administration

The Home Office

Some managers were vaguely dissatisfied –

The Home Office is not of very much help.

while others were somewhat caustic –

We find a good deal of interference from the Home Office by keen idealistic individuals who have had nothing whatever to do personally with actually handling delinquent and maladjusted girls and have no conception of the real problems involved.

Some did not want the Home Office at all –

There is a growing feeling among some approved school staffs that to be logical, approved schools should come under the educational system and not under the Home Office. This removal from the Home Office, however, is against the wishes of the majority of the school managers.

whilst others had only limited criticisms.

Delays

Many managers were emphatic and specific in their criticisms. Foremost amongst these was the problem of delays –

The relationship of school managers with the Home Office leaves much to be desired. At times one feels that the Home Office exists only to place difficulties in one's way; the delays and postponements are intolerable and frustrating.

Policy

Formulation of policy also raised comment –

The division of responsibility for policy between the managers and the Home Office is insufficiently defined at present often leading to frustrating exchanges of letters and visits in both directions.

It will be a good thing when the Home Office has decided upon a definite policy concerning the training of young offenders, recent constant changes of opinion have impeded progress.

Communication

These criticisms are at least party due to an inadequate exchange of information –

The pathetic short-comings seem to be that the Home Office has rich opportunities for amassing experience and information but it is virtually impossible for managers to tap this source. This isolation of managers seems to breed lethargy.

I think it is deplorable that H.M. Inspectors' reports are not made available to managers.

Control

Questions of control were also raised –

Home Office control extends to unnecessary detail.

Finance

Critics of financial arrangements for approved schools were divided between those who disapproved of the system on administrative grounds –

I am appalled at the ludicrous financial arrangements under which the managers have to work.

and those who were resentful of the amount of money spent on the schools –

I consider that public expenditure on the approved schools is unnecessarily lavish.

It must be remembered that we also have a duty to the taxpayer.

There were some concrete suggestions –

A contingency fund . . . to deal with unforeseen and urgent needs . . . would . . . be helpful.

but not all the comments were critical –

The Home Office Inspectorate and other visitors are most helpful and considerate.

and there was also a note of gratitude –

Our school is over one hundred years old and now for the first time we have money, plant and machinery to get ahead with.

Approved schools and their function

The value of approved schools

There were those who were satisfied that the schools were doing a good job –

I feel we are doing all we can under the present régime.

there were those who had some doubts –

I feel that the existing system works but I sometimes doubt that the system is the correct one.

those who had criticisms –

Is our form of training teaching boys how to live in a closed community?

and those who objected to a basic principle –

My personal attitude from experience in this work including Court work is that the herding together of any one type of person is not good.

One view rejected approved schools altogether –

Approved schools in themselves are an anachronism in that we are still in the era of punishing children for apparent misdeeds. Even on taking a very superficial history of these children it is very obvious that their 'crimes' are a reflection of their needs in terms of the family.

Discipline

Comments on discipline expressed concern in only one direction –

I think that there should be rather more discipline and a tougher attitude towards the boys and rather less psychiatric treatment. I also feel that the conditions under which the boys live are too comfortable when compared to the homes to which they have to return.

Psychiatric problems

Although some schools specialize in the treatment of educationally sub-normal children, a number of unsuitable youngsters come into the schools which are not able to cope with them. In addition to mentally or educationally retarded youngsters, children and adolescents with other problems also find their way into approved schools –

Adequate provision in mental hospitals for the treatment of the sick adolescent now frequently and unwisely committed to approved schools [is an urgent requirement].

Boys were seen as a special problem when they were violent –

It is sometimes difficult to deal adequately and immediately with the very violent boy to prevent serious damage to himself, to others and to property.

but this applied even more to the violent and difficult adolescent girl, who is mentioned more frequently –

Not enough girls have been properly classified before being sent to the approved school. A proportion suffer from some mental disorder and are sent to approved schools where the staffs are unable to deal with them. They need mental treatment in a specialized unit.

There are only vague and ill-defined ideas on how psychiatric guidance and treatment can be utilized in the schools –

I am a trained psychiatrist and the school of which I am a manager specializes in giving psychiatric treatment to the girls. My main function is to help from a professional point of view, to advise the management in order to keep a balance between training, education and treatment.

Girls' schools

Managers of girls' approved schools commented on several difficulties related to their tasks. There is the 'incongruity' of having working girls in schools –

In a senior school too much emphasis is put on school. You cannot treat girls of 16–18 as juniors.

the mixture of delinquent with care, protection and control cases –

I doubt if the best use is made of girls' approved schools as long as the mixed intake of girls with a court finding of guilt and girls with a need for care and protection is continued. I feel strongly that they should be educated and treated in different schools.

and the problems of pregnant girls –

A special unit should be set up to receive girls who are committed to approved schools and who are found to be pregnant. I personally feel this would alleviate many difficulties in this connection.

Some comments draw attention to wider social problems –

I believe that so far as adolescent girls are concerned the community needs to be trained rather than or as well as the girls.

and to some characteristics of girls who are admitted –

The girls being received now are considerably more troublesome, absconding and stealing.

There is no doubt that the majority of our girls are all below normal intelligence.

Problems of staffing

Heads of schools

Whilst some managers put their faith and trust in heads of their schools –

I have complete confidence in the headmaster and staff of the school.

others were more critical and insisted on an independent role for managers –

At the moment the schools depend too much on the personality of their headmasters.

co-operation was also envisaged –

As the approved school system is still very much in a state of flux or learning, I think the managers in conjunction with the head should be allowed to try out various ideas which they might have.

Other staff

Many managers express the overriding importance of having the right staff –

In dealing with delinquents wonderful buildings and equipment are quite useless without the right kind of staff with the right personality.

and the extent to which they depend on staff –

Most managers are *not* trained in child welfare, they should work through the staff.

There were some strong views on the value of qualifications –

Academic qualifications [for staff] should be subservient to a vocational call.

and on selection procedures. Difficulties and criticisms include the payment of staff ranging from views that –

Staff of approved schools are grossly underpaid.

to the opposite view that –

Many approved schools are, I feel, over-staffed at great public expense.

There were criticisms of staff attitudes –

No matter how well-meaning staff are, they are still obsessed with the idea of crime and punishment.

and of too much security and self-interest –

Once people are 'in' such a school as this they tend to stick and their capacities are not reviewed by the managers unless positively unsatisfactory.

The problem of supply raised fewer comments than expected –

The two schools of which I am manager are never fully staffed.

Release and after-care

Review

Some managers have described their review methods –

My school has a review sub-committee which sees all boys and decides whether they should be released.

and others have pointed out the snags –

We had a scheme of interviewing all the boys three or four times a year. . . . Unfortunately, owing to shortage of housemasters, these interviews have been brought to an end.

Agents

Some have drawn attention to the need for good after-care
agents –

So much of the value of the work and achievement of the school is
lost because of the lack of good after-care agents.

Homes

Others have pin-pointed the problem of the homes youngsters
go back to –

The biggest headache comes when [girls] are ready for licence and
have to go back to the same home conditions.

I am appalled to realize that we shall probably have to send our
girls back to the insoluble family problems which are why they came
to us.

After-care

Many managers emphasize the importance of after-care –

The main weakness of the present system is in after-care.

The after-care organization is defective and needs attention.

and some had concrete suggestions to make –

Very much more should be done to find suitable employment for
youngsters released on licence.

Schools should have supervision powers after release extended.

Hostels

A large group called for after-care hostels. The demand for
more residential or non-residential after-care was so great that
one might wonder whether there was not an attempt to shift the
treatment process from the school to the post-school period.
After-care would be expected to mean supervision after treatment or training in a school. This emphasis on post-school
treatment might call the justification of the school programme
into question –

The provision of a hostel . . . could be invaluable and allow the boys or girls to find their own feet, having been organized and disciplined for two years or so and then being thrown out to civilian life.

But there were also those who took a gloomier view –

When the position has been reached that between 60 per cent and 65 per cent of young people released from approved schools commit further crimes within two years of release, then clearly the whole of the approved school system needs an urgent review.

Parents of approved-school children

The views of earlier managers find a strange echo on the subject of parents –

If parents were brought to court and punished . . . there would be a worth-while decrease in juvenile delinquency.

The main cause of juvenile deliquency is . . . due to the irresponsibility of parents. Too much emphasis is made today on the reform of the delinquent [than] on the protection of society.

but there were managers who saw this problem differently –

The more co-operation there is between the home and the school then so the chances of eventual success are strengthened.

The liaison with the home is the weakest part of the system at present.

Approved schools and the community

Research

There was support for research –

The reason I would welcome more research is that there seems to be a need for this.

but some of it was qualified by a provision that it be kept out of the schools –

Research is needed but not in the schools.

or some by other reservations –

[research is acceptable] provided that the research is conducted by common-sense people and not by psycho types.

Public morals and public relations

Society at large gets some of the blame for delinquency –

The moral rot within society is not being answered. There are few standards left today so why should we expect them of our children?

There was a widespread conviction that the public knows very little about approved schools –

The general public is incredibly ignorant about the Home Office approved schools system.

There were several comments calling for an improvement in public relations –

I think it might be useful if the function of the approved school was more widely appreciated by the great British public.

but only one comment acknowledged the responsibility of managers for good public relations –

[approved schools] are very frequently confused with detention centres, I think this P.R.O. business is an important function of managers.

This may be due to the existence of diametrically opposed views –

The more public discussions there are the better.

I do not think that a home or a school benefits from public discussions.

Magistrates

Some criticisms were expressed about magistrates in juvenile courts –

Magistrates are unfortunately on the whole disinclined to send delinquent children to an approved school soon enough thereby making the task of the approved school more difficult.

There are times when I am appalled at the heavy hand of the courts in sending the lads to [my] school.

but one manager who is also a magistrate was content –

As a manager and a magistrate I am a great believer in the value of approved schools. I think their success rate is very good.

The position of voluntary managers today

There was a time when voluntary managers were amateurs in a period when this was inevitable because there were no professionals. They had power because they provided the bulk of the necessary finance to establish schools, and authority because they represented unchallenged social values. They were therefore regarded not only as the best people to fill this role but as the only ones. Although the theoretical position of voluntary managers has not changed, everything around them has. Furthermore, they are no longer a uniform body of amateurs but a considerable mixture of amateurs and all levels of professional sophistication. This in itself does not appear to work very well, but the external changes are more far-reaching. We need consider only the most important of these to substantiate our argument.

The source of *finance* in the system will be the source of greatest power and therefore control. Managers today have only a marginal role in securing and administering the financial resources of the approved-school system and many of the inconsistencies in the system spring from this fact.

Because finance comes from central and local government, *control* is largely vested there. A new managing committee or headmaster must, in the first instance, structure a school in accordance with centrally determined rules and regulations. It is my submission that, by the time this has been done, there is very little room left for initiative, originality or independent action. Not enough, at any rate, to make it possible to establish a unit which will differ markedly or in its over-all policy from any other unit. The resultant uniformity is not in the best interests of the schools.

In loco parentis is a legal device which has been maintained throughout although many managers and society at large would no longer accept it as defined by the pioneers of the system. Nor is it likely to be of any value in contemporary child care practice.

Perhaps the most important result arising from this study is that it demonstrates the shift in over-all *authority* in all areas of the system from the managers to the Home Office. This shift was based on the transference of financial responsibility for the schools from the voluntary bodies to the State, and the simultaneous demands by the State to justify the assumption of financial control by assuming control also over those aspects of the system which in the course of time had been shown to be inadequate. The end result is that, while the State has all the authority, the managers still carry the full *responsibility* for the schools, and to the extent that such an arrangement makes the system unworkable the schools are inefficient and ineffective.

Chapter 4

Prerequisites of Change

The foregoing analysis leads to an inescapable conclusion that the approved school system is inadequate to meet the demands made upon it and it would be surprising if, in the circumstances, the system were more successful than it is. In saying this, it should be made clear, however, that it would be less than fair to single out any one group of individuals and assign blame. Many problems facing our schools are historical in origin and organizational in character. Because they are rooted in the structure of the system it would seem to be unlikely that they can be corrected at the local level without simultaneously restructuring the whole. There is now a widely accepted recognition of the need for change, but there may also be a danger of changes being imposed prematurely on individual residential units without a preliminary examination of some basic attitudes which must be altered before change can be made effective.

I have already discussed the need for clearly defined goals especially because there have been conflicts about the goals of correctional institutions for young offenders from their inception. For one thing there is a widely recognized ambivalence in the attitudes of the public to the detention of youngsters. There is an inevitable conflict between goals that are deemed to satisfy the needs of the child and those that are deemed to satisfy the demands for security from the community. Throughout this century, however, the formulation of comprehensible goals for the system has been made more difficult by the growing doubts that have arisen and the questions that have been asked but remain unanswered: Is it right to collect young offenders in large groups and expose them to the risks of sub-cultural conditioning? Do approved schools have a punitive function, and if so how is it to be exercised – if not, what is the justification for providing training or treatment, however badly needed, under conditions of legal detention? Is an approved school an educational establishment, if so why does it detain youngsters beyond school age? Is it a training establishment, if so why does it admit and train youngsters known to be in need of treatment? Is it a treatment unit, if so why do so few of them provide facilities for treatment?

Since 1933 when the distinction between reformatories and industrial schools was abolished, children have been admitted to approved schools either because they are offenders (for training because they are a danger to society), or because they are in need of care, protection or control (for training because they are a danger to themselves). Are these groups sufficiently compatible to make a uniform method of training feasible? And should legal restraints be exercised over both groups?

The role and attitudes of parents of children in approved schools are now widely recognized as being vitally important to the success of any training programme. Does this make the continued compulsory separation of child from parents as meaningful as it was once deliberate?

The increasingly sophisticated classification process used in boys' schools has brought new problems to the fore. On the one hand, it can isolate treatment needs for individual boys which the schools are unable to meet; is it in such cases justifiable to send children to prolonged detention, knowing that by doing so one may be depriving them of the treatment they really need? On the other hand, one is bound to ask what is the justification for subjecting youngsters to extensive classifying procedures when we do not subject our schools to the same processes of analysis of competences and weaknesses, and how reliable is the matching process going to be if only one side of the match has been objectively evaluated?

There is now general agreement about the need for change but, in my view, any change in order to be effective must be preceded by a reconsideration of some of the basic problems which have been described. To begin with, if schools are going to be able to formulate meaningful goals, they must have a clear definition, from the larger society, *of whom the schools are for*. This means a definition of delinquent youngsters which is derived not so much from academic considerations, but which carries clear operational implications for the practitioner.

I TOWARDS AN OPERATIONAL DEFINITION OF DELINQUENCY

There have been many attempts to define delinquency even though all those who have done so have been aware of the difficulties involved in such an attempt. These difficulties lie in the need to incorporate in any definition *what* has been done (the legal view which is liable to change over time and with age), *why* it has been done (criminal intent, psycho-social conscious or unconscious motives), by whom it has been done (the problem of hidden delinquency), the cultural context (whether the child has been socialized to see the act as delinquent), and the treatment implications (how society should deal with the child). The results are not, however, very helpful. There are purely legalistic descriptions: 'An individual who has been or is liable to be brought before a juvenile court either because he has committed a criminal offence or for some other reason within the jurisdiction of the court.'[1] This is also the view of Paul Tappan, expressed twenty years earlier.[2] Other definitions attempt to see delinquency in wider terms. Robison defined it as 'any behaviour which a given community at a given time considers in conflict with its best interests, whether or not the offender has been brought to court'.[3] Martin and Fitzpatrick's definition is even more comprehensive: 'Delinquency is an illegal act, or series of acts, committed by particular children operating in specific motivational-situational-cultural contexts, as they seek to resolve, at different levels of consciousness, par-

---

[1] C. Duncan Mitchell (ed.), *A Dictionary of Sociology*, London, 1968, p. 52.

[2] 'The Juvenile Delinquent is a person who has been adjudicated as such by a court of proper jurisdiction.' See 'The Nature of Juvenile Delinquency' in R. Giallombardo (ed.), *Juvenile Delinquency – a Book of Readings*, New York, 1966, quote from p. 23.

[3] Sophia H. Robison, *Juvenile Delinquency – Its Nature and Control*, New York, 1964, p. 9.

ticular problems with which they are confronted.'[1] Wirt and Briggs also range widely:

... a person whose misbehaviour is a relatively serious legal offence, which is inappropriate to his level of development; it is not committed as a result of extremely low intellect, intracranial organic pathology or severe mental or metabolic dysfunction; and it is alien to the culture in which he has been reared. Whether or not the individual is apprehended or legally adjudicated is not crucial.[2]

Perhaps the widest and most surprising definition comes from Wilkins who stated that delinquency was 'any behaviour on the part of the younger age-groups of the population such that the senior groups object to it'.[3]

Clearly, none of these definitions is of help in formulating goals for treatment or training institutions either because they are at best only research-oriented or because they offer no real help in clarifying the problem of distinguishing between sections of juvenile populations. Some of the concepts we have quoted may possibly be applied to entire child-populations whilst others are highly specific in legal terms.[4]

Our problem is to find a concept which need not be so comprehensive and so inclusive that it can be used at all levels, but which clearly describes a condition in terms of its consequences and social significance. This is what I mean by an *operational* definition. From this standpoint Mary Carpenter's concept is still perhaps the most valuable and the most comprehensive. As I have described earlier, Mary Carpenter held that it was not what the child did that mattered most but *the effect of its own*

[1] J. M. Martin and J. P. Fitzpatrick, *Delinquent Behaviour*, New York, 1964, p. 9.

[2] R. D. Wirt and B. F. Briggs, 'The Meaning of Delinquency' in H. C. Quay (ed.), *Juvenile Delinquency – Research and Theory*, New York, 1965, quote from pp. 23–24.

[3] L. T. Wilkins, 'Juvenile Delinquency: A Critical Review of Research and Theory', *Educ. Research*, 5:2, 1962, pp. 104–119, quote from p. 107. For a good discussion of the problems of definition see W. C. Kvaraceus, *Anxious Youth – Dynamics of Delinquency*, Ohio, 1966.

[4] It is of course inevitable that any definition which attempts to deal with 'hidden delinquency' will be of greater interest to those concerned with prevention rather than treatment. See *Hidden Delinquency* by J. B. Mays, Third National Conference on Research and Teaching in Criminology, Cambridge, 1968.

actions on the child.[1] She preferred to see the behaviour of children in terms of their developmental needs and argued that what mattered most was how a wrong act was dealt with. We know that many, if not most, children do things which could bring them to a juvenile court, but very few actually are so brought. We know that children can be processed by a juvenile court without having committed a wrong act.[2] We know that offenders who have not been brought before a court do not grow up more criminal than those who have, and we know that those who have appeared before a court on non-criminal grounds can be treated and are frequently affected by this process in the same way as those with a finding of guilt against them.[3] What matters, therefore, is that, for whatever reason, a child has been forced beyond the confines of normal interaction levels (i.e. family, school, neighbourhood), and has been brought into interaction with the control forces of the wider society and in doing so, the wider society explicitly challenges the parents' role and competence and places the functions of social control foremost.[4] Our definition of the youngsters coming into approved schools would therefore be *children and young persons in interaction with the control systems of society.*

It could be argued that in such a definition, conflict rather than interaction should be specified, but this is not necessarily so. A child need not be in conflict with social control systems to be sent to an approved school. In fact there are quite a number of children whose conflicts are the result of interaction with social control systems rather than the cause.

---

[1] See Chapter 4, pp. 42–3.

[2] Section 44 (1) of the Children and Young Persons Act, 1933 (23 Geo. 5, Ch. 12) refers to children brought before a juvenile court 'either as being in need of care or protection or as an offender or otherwise'. Section 2 (1) of the Children and Young Persons Act, 1963, refers to 'such care, protection and guidance as a good parent [sic!] may reasonably be expected to give'.

[3] 60 per cent girls and 5 per cent boys in approved schools were committed under care, protection or control proceedings. See statistics relating to *Approved Schools, Remand Homes and Attendance Centres in England and Wales*, 1966, H.M.S.O., 441, 1967.

[4] Thus although Section 44 (1), op. cit., admonishes the court to 'have regard to the welfare of the child or young person', it also specifies 'steps for removing him from undesirable surroundings and for securing that proper provision is made for his education and training'.

2 THE VALIDITY OF THE HOSPITAL MODEL

In 1853 Mary Carpenter described principles for the treatment of 'morally diseased' children to bring them into a 'sound and healthy state'.[1] Sydney Turner too saw the function of a reformatory as a 'hospital to cure real disease'.[2] This view of young offenders as in some way diseased and requiring a specific form of treatment in a hospital-type institution has persisted although the terminology has to some extent changed. We are now more likely to talk of wayward, maladjusted, disturbed or damaged children but the basic idea remains the same, that approved schools deal with youngsters who are partially diseased in such a way that the treatment of their disorder must take precedence over any other provisions that we would make for them. This means moral hospitals[3] or treatment units or therapeutic communities as the kinds of institutions which are necessary to carry out this task.

While there is no doubt that a proportion of those committed to approved schools display social or psychological pathologies which demand more or less sophisticated professional skills for their management, this nevertheless leaves unexamined the fundamental question of the justification for concentrating, in the provisions offered, on those areas where the youngster has shown apparent disturbances. We thereby create in the minds of the youngster, those who deal with him, and the community at large, the idea that we are concerned with individuals so abnormal as to be unlike and fundamentally different from all other children. If this were true it would justify his isolation on the hospital model, but apart from that such an approach appears to be only negative in its consequences. The youngster sees himself in the way he is labelled, as being in conflict with society. He is forced to seek models for identification amongst similarly segregated deviant peers and he is denied the opportunity to work through normal developmental difficulties in a normal and familiar environment.

All this in spite of strong evidence that the majority of

[1] *Juvenile Delinquents*, op. cit., p. 292.
[2] Cf. *Second Report Inspector of Reformatory Schools*, 1859, p. 19.
[3] Cf. The Earl of Lytton, 'Moral Hospitals', *Howard J.*, 2:2, 1927, pp. 88–93.

Mc

juvenile delinquents are delinquent more because they are juvenile than because of any inherent criminal traits; and the problematic value of our present forms of approved school training, viewed at a national level, would appear to be counter-productive if the re-conviction rate for the schools as a whole remains at 62 per cent of those admitted.[1]

Closely related to the concept of the diseased child that has to be specially treated is the idea of the tainted parent whose ignorance, incapacity or criminality has contributed to the condition of the child. Throughout the nineteenth century it was axiomatic that the child must be removed from its environment and that the institution must become the new and better family in which the child was to be reared. In spite of the growing emphasis on the importance of the parents in the approved school programmes, the punitive approach towards them remains deeply entrenched, in both the legal framework and in the operations of the schools themselves.[2] Here again it is not my intention to deny or to belittle the importance of the effects inadequate parents may have on their children and the frequency with which unsatisfactory home conditions can be demonstrated to be the link with deviant and neurotic behaviour in approved-school intakes.[3] It seems to me, however, that it is inevitable that where a child's parents and background are called into question this will produce negative results on the child, who is unlikely to experience the social rejection of his parents without serious consequences to his self-esteem and self-respect.

A third element in the Victorian conception of the moral hospital, which remains rooted in present-day provisions, concerns the economic considerations governing the establishment of treatment centres. If there are a number of persons whose

---

[1] Although the approved schools put the blame for the persistence of punitive attitudes on the general public, they have done little to introduce internal changes to counter them. Cf., *Approved Schools and the Future*, Monograph No. 7, Association of Headmasters, Headmistresses and Matrons of Approved Schools, 1955.

[2] Thus home leave is subject to a boy's behaviour and the 'suitability' of the home. Correspondence with and visits by parents are subject to the headmaster's approval. See *Approved School Rules*, 1949 (No. 2052).

[3] See Julius Carlebach, 'Families of Delinquents and the Approved Schools', *Approved Schools Gazette*, 59:11, 1966, pp. 447–53.

condition threatens the general community and requires specialized care, then the cheapest way of satisfying both these aspects is to set aside a large (and therefore cheap) and relatively isolated (and therefore safe) institution which will meet the situation. A substantial proportion of our approved schools are still in fairly isolated positions mainly in rural areas, even though a majority of approved-school youngsters come from densely populated urban areas. Approved schools are not perhaps as large, particularly in the case of girls, as they used to be, but many of them are still large enough to create and sustain intense deviant sub-cultures to which a considerable proportion of their members are bound to succumb. Some of the factors responsible for this have already been discussed, but a widespread unawareness or lack of enlightened policies in the use of socialization techniques also contributes to this.

A child enters a residential unit with a complex system of social norms which, to the extent that they were acquired from infancy onwards, are closely interwoven with his emotional attachments and his personal identity. By definition the young delinquent entering an institution is presumed to have a faulty system of social norms and the institution is required to eliminate this and to superimpose another more closely geared to the values and demands of the society to which the youngster will eventually return. There are three ways in which this has been done. Most Victorian institutions kept new admissions in a state of total isolation, thus creating a vacuum in which the value system of the inmate was expected to wither away because all points of reference for exercising it had been eliminated. The effectiveness of this process can be gauged from the fact that in the case of adults it was observed that after some months it led to the total destruction of personality; hence Joshua Jebb reduced the prescribed eighteen months isolation period for prisoners sentenced to penal servitude to nine months. In the case of boys admitted to Parkhurst the period of total isolation was reduced, ameliorated by occasional association with other boys and avoided altogether in the case of younger boys.[1]

The second method, and one still in use in institutions for young offenders today, is a complete denial of the value system

[1] See Julius Carlebach, 'Sir Joshua Jebb 1793–1863', *Prison Service J.*, 4:15 1965, pp. 18–30.

and its emotional antecedents of the new admission. The institution, by coercion and threat, imposes its own value system and accepts superficial conformity as a reasonable form of behaviour. Because the youngster's value system is so closely interwoven with his emotional make-up he seeks reassurance and support for his identity by turning to the inmate sub-cultural group which, in return for adherence to its own norms, will accept and support the youngster's self-concepts.[1]

The third method is the one demonstrated by the 'progressive' residential units and is implicit in the work of men like Lennhoff, Lyward, and Wills.[2] The approach in these residential units is based on complete acceptance and this includes the social value system of the youngster. In the initial period in the institution he is permitted to act out and demonstrate his value system, and it is not until he has established meaningful relationships with one or more members of staff in the unit, that he is expected to first explore and subsequently internalize new social values. To the extent that he does so the institution may be regarded as having been successful.

It is argued, then, that three factors which were ones accepted as basic by Victorian reformers have been largely retained yet, at the very least, demand close re-examination before their continuance is incorporated in any future changes. These factors are that; one, young offenders are in some way diseased; two, that this was in some way due to their parents; three, that for their own and the community's sake they must be removed to a suitable place for treatment.

If it is accepted that the hospital model is inappropriate, at any rate for most of the children in approved schools, then this would carry certain implications for any future development. These are: (a) that the fact that we are dealing with young people demands that any provisions made for them must always

[1] This might be an answer to critics of Clemmer's 'prisonization' concept because it offers a reason *why* the prison culture exists. There is also support in Wheeler's finding that amongst prisoners 'the dominant tendency is to move in the direction of non-conformity rather than isolation'. 'Socialization in Correctional Communities' by Stanton Wheeler, *Amer. Social Review*, 26, 1961, pp. 697–712.

[2] Cf. F. G. Lennhoff, *Exceptional Children*, 2nd Ed. London, 1966. M. Burns, *Mr. Lyward's Answer*, London, 1964. W. D. Wills, *The Barnes Experiment*, London, 1948.

be, first and foremost, normal educational provisions which are concerned as much if not more with ordinary developmental processes as they are with incidental treatment provisions; (b) that unsatisfactory parents or unsatisfactory surroundings are not sufficient reason for depriving most children of their natural environments, though this does not preclude us from offering alternate physical care; (c) in line with our definition of delinquency I would say that most children in interaction with the control systems of society can and should be managed through normal community channels and not through special agencies which were designed to control adult forms of deviant behaviour. Only where normal community channels have failed would more serious intervention be justified.

To make these suggestions more concrete we would first have to divide the population under discussion into those who are at school and those who are beyond school leaving age. For obvious reasons I would like to concentrate on those youngsters who are still at school at the time of their committal, and the proposed outline suggests two possible alternatives in their management if it has been decided that their needs demand removal from their own homes. The first possibility is to attach small residential wings to ordinary day schools. Any child that could not receive adequate physical care in his home would be offered residential care in his school so that none of the child's social and emotional relationships would be severed or seriously interfered with. Teachers and local welfare workers could then, in a very real sense, act as aides to the child and his parents without introducing the inevitable punitive note which complete removal even for remand purposes carries with it.[1]

The second alternative for youngsters needing more substantial care and more specific forms of treatment would be the provision of State boarding schools to which those over the age of thirteen could be sent. These schools need not be in close proximity to the child's home but they would see themselves and represent themselves to the child and his parents as primarily educational institutions whose main goal and aim is to offer the child an education that would enable him to realize his potential and to stimulate maximum growth.

[1] See also Barbara Wootton, 'Children in Trouble', the *Observer*, 29 August 1965.

Unfortunately, it will probably still be necessary to have a few maximum security institutions which will have to operate as much to contain the youngsters committed to them as to provide them with education, but when the previously described alternatives are available it should be possible to reduce the number of those in maximum security units to a bare minimum and restrict it only to those who really need it.

It is only when normal educational provisions accept full responsibility for educating and assisting even those who have shown some difficulty or who have strayed from the 'path of righteousness' that we will be able to concentrate our resources, financial and manpower, to offer specialized care to those who *ought* to have it.

3 THE NEED FOR LEADERSHIP

It is not possible to deal at length with problems of leadership even if one felt competent to do so. We are concerned here only with those aspects of the subject which arise directly from the historical analysis and which have a bearing on any future change.

I have already stated that the care of children with special needs is an act of faith which no amount of professional skill and expertise makes superfluous. The individual who wants to guide and help must do so from an inner conviction that he has the capacity to accept the unacceptable, to lead the uncertain, to inspire the defeated and to encourage the hopeless. But he also needs knowledge, the ability to distinguish between innovation and well-tried formulae, between meaningful change and superficial alteration, between real needs and assumed ones. He must understand not only the youngsters he cares for, the staff who assist him and the tasks which are relevant to this, but also the institution which is his operational framework and the society which relies on his activities as an integral part of social health. He must have skills, for the management of people and organizations is too complex to be encompassed within one person's life experiences, and whilst he must always be aware of the necessity to learn, this learning should not be too often or too dangerously at the expense of those he is charged to care for.

To put this more briefly, to be a leader of a residential unit for children a man must know what he is doing, he must believe in what he is doing, and he must be able to formulate and to communicate his aims, his motives and his methods. This would seem to me to be the crucial test of effective unit control. It would appear, however, that very few heads of approved schools have demonstrated a capacity for satisfying these criteria, though this may be due as much to 'hierarchical asphyxiation' as to poor selection.

It is not only the immediate head of a unit who must show a genuine capacity for leadership. Effective leadership must be felt throughout the system from the supervisory level (inspectorate), through the administrative level (local authority or voluntary management) to the individual unit. Our study shows clearly that a forceful and even controversial and, above all, conspicuous chief inspector inspires more thought, activity and reform than the most conscientious, anonymous and silent civil servant. Whatever forms the provisions for delinquent children may finally assume, they will always be a part of the society which authorizes and creates them and it should therefore be an integral function of leadership to ensure that the community is and remains involved in the tasks and objectives of its own institutions. Neither public scandal nor the bitterest controversy are likely to be as harmful as silence and public apathy where residential units are intended to prepare their charges for living in society and not just withdrawing them from it.

4 CHILDREN IN TROUBLE

Finally, we might briefly consider the proposals contained in the most recent Government White Paper as far as they are relevant to our discussions, although it should perhaps be stressed that the very brevity of that paper makes many of the ideas and concepts it contains somewhat obscure and even ambiguous.[1]

In line with our suggested definition of delinquents as children in interaction with the control system of society, the changes relating to juvenile court procedures (paras. 14–16), which

---

[1] Home Office, *Children in Trouble*, H.M.S.O., 1968, Cmnd. 3601.

abolish prosecutions of children aged 10–14 years and restrict prosecutions of young offenders aged 14–17 years, are very welcome. It should be noted, however, that, as Scott has pointed out, there is nothing in the White Paper to suggest that the implications of such changes in relation to court assessments and the training and definition of function of magistrates have been examined.[1] The promised emphasis on keeping as many children as possible in homes to be established 'on a genuine local basis' (para. 36) is equally to be welcomed but there are in this writer's view[2] a number of recommendations which are still so deeply rooted in tradition and so inappropriate to the needs of children that they are likely to be either harmful or organizationally ineffective.

(a) The perpetuation of the 'good parent' idea (para. 14). This is little more than a modernized version of the punitive approach to parents which has already been described. Who can say what constitutes a good parent, a concept so heavily dependent on questions of social class, ethnic group and economic capacity, or chance? How far will a court decision that parents are not providing such care as might 'reasonably be expected' from a 'good parent', reflect a child's view of its parents? Come to that, what useful purpose would be served by calling the quality of parental care into question at all? We do not require a court to rule parents as educationally inadequate in order to compel a child to attend an ordinary school; why then should we not operate on the same basis if we wish to extend educational provisions in accordance with the child's special (or extraordinary) needs?

(b) Closely related to this attitude towards parents is the definition of the function of children's homes which, it is stated, 'will operate as nearly as possible in the same way as a good family' (para. 31). This once again implies that children who need parental care also need parental substitution, although the evidence, as far as it exists, would seem to point to an opposite

---

[1] P. D. Scott, 'Children in Trouble: A New Government White Paper', *Brit. J. Crim.*, 8:3, 1968, pp. 309–12.

[2] Which would appear to be supported by the newly published, *Report of the Committee on Local Authority and Allied Personal Services*, H.M.S.O., 1968, Cmnd. 3703 (The Seebohm Committee Report).

conclusion. Most children in residential units, including approved schools, remain there for relatively short periods, and the majority of them return to their normal homes. Even in specifically therapeutic settings it is recognized that, though children may have to be offered opportunities for primary experiences, this does not necessarily demand the provision of a new primary group. Even to attempt to displace the natural family, therefore, is a measure which should only be applied for children who have a demonstrable need for this and it is very doubtful if this is likely for any substantial proportion of those actually in residential care.

(c) There are also comments and proposals which suggest an attitude to children in care which we have met frequently in our historical analysis, but which in spite of well-intentioned motives are damaging in their effect. Comments like aiming to return children to 'normal services' and keeping more children in units where 'the first priority will be a therapeutic approach to social education' (para. 31), imply an unawareness of children's developmental needs, and place the control function of residential units above their educational role, in situations where this does not appear to be justified. The old hospital model that has been described is very much to the fore when *therapy* is advocated for *social* education. As I have tried to stress earlier, unless a youngster is so seriously ill that he cannot benefit even from specialized educational facilities (and that applies to very few approved-school boys and girls) it is difficult to see the purpose and justification for creating separate and segregated units which will contribute as much to the youngsters deviant self-concept as they will to his 'normalization'.

(d) There is a call for 'centres for observation and assessment' to provide the 'best possible diagnosis' (para. 33). This can be valuable and important but only if it is related first to the professional competence of those who make and use the assessments; secondly, if it is properly co-ordinated with the assessment and evaluation of the facilities which are being offered; and, thirdly, if it is justified as a means for contributing to a decision-making process which is genuinely geared to the needs of the child. At the moment this is not always the case. In child

care the process of assessment is too often followed by a place-
ment determined by available vacancies rather than child
need. In the approved schools the classification process can be
futile and harmful when neither the schools nor their staffs are
organized and specialized in a way that would give treatment
proposals arising from classification some meaning. There is
always the danger that a child becomes a product to be manipu-
lated rather than a person to be assisted. The power to assess
a child must carry with it the appropriate responsibility for the
child as a person.

Taking the section 'Residential Treatment' (pp. 11–12) as a
whole, there appears to be no reason why the provisions
discussed under this heading could not and should not be
encompassed in our present, though broadened, day- and
boarding-school services.

(e) In the field of residential provisions the most important
innovation of the White Paper is the creation of 'community
homes', and it is a pity that this important concept has not been
properly developed. A community home could be one or all of
three things. It could be a home run as a community; it could
be a home established by a community as a part of that community; or it could be a home established for the reception of
those who are to be separated from the community. There is no
indication how this concept is visualized, unless of course we
take the earlier description of a children's home as being like a
good family. Could this include the role of a community home
as being a home run on partial self-government lines in which
children can participate meaningfully in decisions that affect
their lives and activities? There is clearly a need for a very
precise definition and one can only hope that when it is put
forward it will strongly underline both of the first two possibili-
ties which have been suggested, namely, that it will be a unit
run on community lines and established by and closely inter-
twined with the local community in which it is situated. There
appear to be no reasons why such community homes should not
be natural extensions of local schools. The real danger
which false definition involves is that community homes
will become twentieth-century versions of Victorian workhouses.

(f) It is not surprising, but nevertheless unfortunate, that the management and inspection of residential units are to be continued as at present with very little regard to the unsatisfactory nature of contemporary management concepts and the irrelevancies of traditional methods of inspection. There is no mention of a re-definition of managerial function in residential units, and there is no hint that advanced techniques of consultation and professional guidance will replace the traditional patterns of supervision and inspection; yet both of these are essential if the residential care of young people is to be given new meaning, and if the professional needs of the services are to be brought in line with the methods and techniques that the increasing levels of staff training will demand.

As a final comment we might note that whilst the White Paper pays a great deal of attention to what might be done to and with children, it entirely ignores the desperate problem of role definitions and unit leadership. The administrative superstructures to be imposed on residential units are to be increased and extended, and it is difficult to see how effective unit leadership can be provided for in a system so burdened by 'hierarchical asphyxiation'. There is in the White Paper a genuine desire to improve and professionalize the services we offer to our children. One can only hope that this desire will be coupled with a flexibility and freshness that will make the helping processes what they ought to be.

Chapter 5

Theoretical Suggestions for Future Research

I

The most difficult problem in this study has been to find a frame of reference for describing and analysing a system which can be characterized as much by its internal uniformity as by sub-system variability.

The approved school system is a closed system in the sense that, so far, it has functioned with very little reference to allied and associated areas of child care and has carefully avoided identification with the penal system. It looks to highly formalized channels (Home Office, managers' association, heads' association, etc.) to represent its interests and to protect its status in the community. One result of this is an almost complete intolerance of criticisms which, even at relatively sophisticated levels, tend to be regarded, interpreted and treated as personal attacks and denial of the worth of individuals. Even at governmental level it is sometimes difficult to demonstrate that a school or sub-unit can be 'bad' (i.e. inefficient and ineffective) for reasons which need not be associated with the quality of the staff. This makes it all the more important to find some basis for critical analysis, which is demonstrably independent of personality variables. Two approaches which have been tried will be of interest here. The first is Goffman's famous model of the 'total institution'. Goffman argued that residential units if treated as sociological entities have so much in common, that certain behaviour in both staff and inmates, and certain effects on them, must be regarded as *inherent* in residential institutions, and have 'good functional reasons' for their existence.[1] He

[1] Erving Goffman, op. cit., p. 124.

180

described the characteristics of total institutions under four main headings to justify his claim that institutions were 'social hybrids', being part residential community and part formal organization.

1 In total institutions normal barriers separating the sleep–play–work cycle of the individual are broken down.
2 There is a basic split between two separate groups in each institution – inmates and staff.
3 Work has a different meaning from the normal work-payment structure in the larger society.
4 People live in batches instead of in families.[1]

Goffman thus sees the importance of the residential unit in the structural differences between it and social life in a normal society.

It is quite possible that a systematic comparison of extended family systems with residential units would lead to rather different conclusions. The same may be argued for comparisons of social systems based on barter or subsistence economies with residential units.

There are also other difficulties in Goffman's analysis. His concept of the 'total' institution is rather vague, for it would have meaning only if it could be shown that a progressive decrease in 'totality' will bring about a progressive decrease in the effects of 'totality'. But this is not so. In the approved schools, for example, some of the manifestations of totality have been deliberately removed (note for example the growing emphasis on maintaining *close* contact between a boy and his home), but there is no real evidence that this has been reflected in lesser 'disculturation' or less severe 'destruction of the self'. What we would have to argue, therefore, is that Goffman's observations can be explained at two levels. (a) They describe individual reactions to social systems which are quite independent of residential units; (b) that the effects described are due not so much to what the institution does to create them, as to the institution's failure to prevent them by positive measures to create opposite effects. It would have to be demonstrated that residential units, which set out to eliminate 'totality' effects by adopting preventive techniques, are unworkable as residential

[1] Goffman, op. cit., pp. 5–12.

organizations before Goffman's hypothesis could be substantiated.

The second approach is to apply organizational theory to residential systems as was done by Etzioni[1] and Lambert.[2] This approach is more attractive because it deals with systems which if not equivalent to the approved schools are at least similar.

Much of what is contained in this type of model could be applied directly to approved schools, but as a frame of reference it fails on the crucial question of organizational goals. Thus Etzioni assumes 'clear and explicit' goals for the educational institutions he describes, which he summarizes as 'the inculcation of knowledge, skills and values'. Lambert has made a three-dimensional structure-function analysis of public-school goals. He divided Etzioni's group into instrumental (knowledge-skills), expressive (values) and organizational (maintenance of the school as an organization) goals. Functionally he saw these as having to be analysed as stated, real and perceived goals. In the case of the approved schools, however, the nature of their goals appear to be much more complex, not least because they are almost by definition contradictory. They also have to be 'multi-functional', that is to say, the goals of approved schools are not 'clear and explicit', but rather are they products of complex social pressures all of which must find expression in the ultimate formulation of goals.[3]

[1] Amitai Etzioni, 'The Organizational Structure of "Closed" Educational Institutions in Israel', *Harvard Educ. Rev.*, 27:2, 1957, pp. 107–125.

[2] Royston Lambert, *A Sociological Introduction to G. Kalton's 'The Public Schools'*, London, 1966.

[3] This is not a new problem but it has, so far, been dealt with in the penal setting which is not really appropriate to approved schools. Thus Ohlin's 'correctional interest groups' differ from goal-formulating levels in our setting. Galtung's 'dilemma' again applies only to prison. See L. E. Ohlin, 'Conflicting Interests in Correctional Objectives' in *Theoretical Studies in Social Organization of the Prison*, Soc. Sc. Res. Council Pamphlet 15, New York, 1960. J. Galtung, 'Prison: The Organization of Dilemma' in D. R. Cressey (Ed.), *The Prison – Studies in Institutional Organization and Change*. A brief review of the problem is presented by D. Blomberg in *The Effectiveness of Punishment and other Measures of Treatment*, Council of Europe, 1967, pp. 169–172. Street, Vinter and Perrow deal with this question in the context of units for juveniles but these are again explicitly correctional. See *Organization for Treatment*, New York, 1966, esp. pp. 13–14.

Residential units are social organizations and, as such, are subject to the characteristics of organizations. They will have to deal with problems of input programmes and output, of control, socialization, leadership and communication. These problems are *inherent* in social organizations and will, inevitably, influence the definition of goals for the unit.

Residential units tend to restrict their intake to specific categories having specific needs (e.g. delinquent, crippled, boy, girl). The *specific* nature of the unit will therefore play a role in the formulation of goals.

Residential units will be part and parcel of a wider social system which can be involved at three levels. The unit may be the product of social policy. It may be subject to public supervision and control. It will be a part of a given neighbourhood. All these involvements are *external* to the actual unit but are nevertheless, wholly or in part, influential in defining unit goals.

Residential units are constantly faced with making or accepting decisions relating to their function and viability. Once a decision has been translated into action it becomes part of unit function and very often survives the situation which originally gave rise to the decision. In this sense, residential units have *traditional* features, which need not necessarily be meaningful in terms of their operation.

These four factors, inherent, specific, external, and traditional, are the bases on which the goals of residential units can be analysed. In the case of approved schools it will be seen from this study that many of the contradictions and conflicts surrounding the schools can be explained by showing the paradoxical influences of these factors in the formulation of school and system goals.

That approved schools are social organizations and have to resolve problems of management, efficiency and effectiveness has yet to be fully accepted at all levels of the system. So far management is still a confused mixture of amateur good-will, administrative skill and professional expertise. There are no meaningful role-definitions for the various levels of authority; aids like cost-effectiveness or operational research are warded off as 'inappropriate' and 'inhuman', hierarchical structures tend to be authoritarian and control is mainly coercive-utilitarian rather than normative, not because these are preferred methods of control but because there is little apparent understanding of the nature of control.

The specific character of approved schools can be defined by emphasizing either that they are dealing with young people or that they are dealing with offenders. The very separateness of the system makes it clear that approved schools have always emphasized the offender side of their intake, and that consequently, they have always been more important as instruments of social control than as units geared primarily to satisfy the developmental needs of their intake. (The schools themselves have always denied being punitive but have not emphasized their educational role either.)

Both the inherent and the specific features of approved schools might thus be expected to contribute mainly in a negative sense to any formulation of goals. More important are the influences of external factors which operate, as I have suggested, at a three-dimensional level. Although originally private and philanthropic undertakings, the schools are used to enhance social control, and as such, are subject to fluctuations and changes in social policy. At Home Office level those things which are frequently claimed as being the *aims* of the system are in reality *methods* of control.[1] At the highest level, the interests of the schools must be balanced against the interests of the larger society. Goals, therefore, would be defined for social equilibrium rather than the absolute acceptance of one interest or another.

At the second external level (managers, including local authorities) goal-definition will depend largely on the availability of resources and the need to assign priorities in their disposal, while at the third (neighbourhood) level more basic

[1] 'Readjustment and Social Re-education', cf. *The Sentence of the Court*, A Handbook for Courts on the Treatment of Offenders, H.M.S.O. Revised ed., 1966, para. 54, p. 13.

problems such as the behaviour of inmates and the relationships between school and community will be decisive.

Astride these influences on goal-definition will be the impact of the traditional factors which in the case of the approved schools are, if anything, the most dominant. This is due mainly, as has been shown, to what might be called the 'Barnacle effect'. The many changes that have been introduced within and relating to the system have rarely been accompanied by a realistic abolition of existing practices. As a result the system is, in many areas, bedevilled by traditional goals and traditional practices which are not only a handicap, but frequently inimical to the effective introduction of reform.

IV

The executive force in each school ought to be the headmaster, who must formulate school aims and school methods which will meet the demands of all pressures and influences which have been described. (There are a number of managers who would reject this and who regard the formulation of school policy as a specific function of management.) It is not perhaps surprising that there are few instances in which this has been successful. It would seem that the Head most likely to conceptualize and execute a meaningful policy will begin, or move outside the system, to free himself from this welter of conflicting demands.

What then of the school whose Head fails to formulate meaningful goals for his organization? The task, as we have seen, is to co-ordinate multiple factors rather than choose between them but if, as I have suggested, most Heads are unable to fulfil this task, what effect will this have on individual schools and the system as a whole? The problem is this. The complexity of goal-definitions may fail to provide working goals for the unit. The unit is left with conflicting aims which lead inevitably to confusion and uncertainty of treatment. A situation in fact which is so reminiscent of a state of anomie that one is tempted to try Merton's model as a theoretical guide. Because the institution has distorted goals which are incorrectly derived from external sources (i.e. the larger social structure) we would opine that *the residential unit itself* is in a state of anomie in relation to the wider goals for the unit in society. If this is true then we ought to expect the unit itself to react in the way Merton has stipulated for individuals in a similar situation. Using Merton's classification we would then have the following:

1 *Conformity:* The unit has integrated goals and thus reflects the goals of the wider society. It is also an effective unit.
2 *Innovation:* The unit defines its own goals and creates its own means for achieving these without alienating its members from the wider society when this is done by the formal leadership of the unit. If informal leadership is responsible for innovations, deviant values are likely to predominate.
3 *Ritualism:* Perhaps the most common reaction. Without goals which link it directly to the social system, the unit formulates and concentrates on internal activities; i.e. expressive activities absorb and displace instrumental activities.
4 *Retreatism:* The unit which specifically rejects cultural goals and formulates its own as a means of dissociating itself from the wider society.
5 *Rebellion:* Informal and subordinate leadership tries to wrest control from formal leadership that is felt to have failed, without any real desire to formulate new goals.

It is an interesting feature of such a theoretical formulation that it offers a convincing structure for Goffman's 'total' institutions which we would now describe as anomic units reacting in a ritualistic or retreatist way to their unsatisfactory goal structure. But it would then also appear that in other forms of reaction there is an implicit defence against becoming a 'total institution'.

Index of Names

Index of Subjects

The International Library of
Sociology
and Social Reconstruction

Edited by W. J. H. SPROTT
Founded by KARL MANNHEIM

ROUTLEDGE & KEGAN PAUL
BROADWAY HOUSE, CARTER LANE, LONDON, E.C.4

CONTENTS

PRINTED IN GREAT BRITAIN BY HEADLEY BROTHERS LTD
109 KINGSWAY LONDON W C 2 AND ASHFORD KENT

GENERAL SOCIOLOGY

Brown, Robert. Explanation in Social Science. *208 pp. 1963. (2nd Impression 1964.) 25s.*

Gibson, Quentin. The Logic of Social Enquiry. *240 pp. 1960. (3rd Impression 1968.) 24s.*

Homans, George C. Sentiments and Activities: Essays in Social Science. *336 pp. 1962. 32s.*

Isajiw, Wsevelod W. Causation and Functionalism in Sociology. *165 pp. 1968. 25s.*

Johnson, Harry M. Sociology: a Systematic Introduction. *Foreword by Robert K. Merton. 710 pp. 1961. (5th Impression 1968.) 42s.*

Mannheim, Karl. Essays on Sociology and Social Psychology. *Edited by Paul Keckskemeti. With Editorial Note by Adolph Lowe. 344 pp. 1953. (2nd Impression 1966.) 32s.*

Systematic Sociology: An Introduction to the Study of Society. *Edited by J. S. Erös and Professor W. A. C. Stewart. 220 pp. 1957. (3rd Impression 1967.) 24s.*

Martindale, Don. The Nature and Types of Sociological Theory. *292 pp. 1961. (3rd Impression 1967.) 35s.*

Maus, Heinz. A Short History of Sociology. *234 pp. 1962. (2nd Impression 1965.) 28s.*

Myrdal, Gunnar. Value in Social Theory: A Collection of Essays on Methodology. *Edited by Paul Streeten. 332 pp. 1958. (3rd Impression 1968.) 35s.*

Ogburn, William F., and **Nimkoff, Meyer F.** A Handbook of Sociology. *Preface by Karl Mannheim. 656 pp. 46 figures. 35 tables. 5th edition (revised) 1964. 45s.*

Parsons, Talcott, and **Smelser, Neil J.** Economy and Society: A Study in the Integration of Economic and Social Theory. *362 pp. 1956. (4th Impression 1967.) 35s.*

Rex, John. Key Problems of Sociological Theory. *220 pp. 1961. (4th Impression 1968.) 25s.*

Stark, Werner. The Fundamental Forms of Social Thought. *280 pp. 1962. 32s.*

FOREIGN CLASSICS OF SOCIOLOGY

Durkheim, Emile. Suicide. A Study in Sociology. *Edited and with an Introduction by George Simpson. 404 pp. 1952. (4th Impression 1968.) 35s.*

Professional Ethics and Civic Morals. *Translated by Cornelia Brookfield. 288 pp. 1957. 30s.*

Gerth, H. H., and **Mills, C. Wright.** From Max Weber: Essays in Sociology. *502 pp. 1948. (6th Impression 1967.) 35s.*

Tönnies, Ferdinand. Community and Association. *(Gemeinschaft und Gesellschaft.) Translated and Supplemented by Charles P. Loomis. Foreword by Pitirim A. Sorokin. 334 pp. 1955. 28s.*

3

SOCIAL STRUCTURE

Andreski, Stanislav. Military Organization and Society. *Foreword by Professor A. R. Radcliffe-Brown. 226 pp. 1 folder. 1954. Revised Edition 1968. 35s.*

Cole, G. D. H. Studies in Class Structure. *220 pp. 1955. (3rd Impression 1964.) 21s. Paper 10s. 6d.*

Coontz, Sydney H. Population Theories and the Economic Interpretation. *202 pp. 1957. (3rd Impression 1968.) 28s.*

Coser, Lewis. The Functions of Social Conflict. *204 pp. 1956. (3rd Impression 1968.) 25s.*

Dickie-Clark, H. F. Marginal Situation: A Sociological Study of a Coloured Group. *240 pp. 11 tables. 1966. 40s.*

Glass, D. V. (Ed.). Social Mobility in Britain. *Contributions by J. Berent, T. Bottomore, R. C. Chambers, J. Floud, D. V. Glass, J. R. Hall, H. T. Himmelweit, R. K. Kelsall, F. M. Martin, C. A. Moser, R. Mukherjee, and W. Ziegel. 420 pp. 1954. (4th Impression 1967.) 45s.*

Jones, Garth N. Planned Organizational Change: An Exploratory Study Using an Empirical Approach. *About 268 pp. 1969. 40s.*

Kelsall, R. K. Higher Civil Servants in Britain: From 1870 to the Present Day. *268 pp. 31 tables. 1955. (2nd Impression 1966.) 25s.*

König, René. The Community. *232 pp. Illustrated. 1968. 35s.*

Lawton, Denis. Social Class, Language and Education. *192 pp. 1968. (2nd Impression 1968.) 25s.*

McLeish, John. The Theory of Social Change: Four Views Considered. *About 128 pp. 1969. 21s.*

Marsh, David C. The Changing Social Structure in England and Wales, 1871-1961. *1958. 272 pp. 2nd edition (revised) 1966. (2nd Impression 1967.) 35s.*

Mouzelis, Nicos. Organization and Bureaucracy. An Analysis of Modern Theories. *240 pp. 1967. (2nd Impression 1968.) 28s.*

Ossowski, Stanislaw. Class Structure in the Social Consciousness. *210 pp. 1963. (2nd Impression 1967.) 25s.*

SOCIOLOGY AND POLITICS

Barbu, Zevedei. Democracy and Dictatorship: Their Psychology and Patterns of Life. *300 pp. 1956. 28s.*

Crick, Bernard. The American Science of Politics: Its Origins and Conditions. *284 pp. 1959. 32s.*

Hertz, Frederick. Nationality in History and Politics: A Psychology and Sociology of National Sentiment and Nationalism. *432 pp. 1944. (5th Impression 1966.) 42s.*

Kornhauser, William. The Politics of Mass Society. *272 pp. 20 tables. 1960. (3rd Impression 1968.) 28s.*

Laidler, Harry W. History of Socialism. Social-Economic Movements: An Historical and Comparative Survey of Socialism, Communism, Co-operation, Utopianism; and other Systems of Reform and Reconstruction. *New edition. 992 pp. 1968. 90s.*

Lasswell, Harold D. Analysis of Political Behaviour. An Empirical Approach. *324 pp. 1947. (4th Impression 1966.) 35s.*

Mannheim, Karl. Freedom, Power and Democratic Planning. *Edited by Hans Gerth and Ernest K. Bramstedt. 424 pp. 1951. (3rd Impression 1968.) 42s.*

Mansur, Fatma. Process of Independence. *Foreword by A. H. Hanson. 208 pp. 1962. 25s.*

Martin, David A. Pacificism: an Historical and Sociological Study. *262 pp. 1965. 30s.*

Myrdal, Gunnar. The Political Element in the Development of Economic Theory. *Translated from the German by Paul Streeten. 282 pp. 1953. (4th Impression 1965.) 25s.*

Polanyi, Michael. F.R.S. The Logic of Liberty: Reflections and Rejoinders. *228 pp. 1951. 18s.*

Verney, Douglas V. The Analysis of Political Systems. *264 pp. 1959. (3rd Impression 1966.) 28s.*

Wootton, Graham. The Politics of Influence: British Ex-Servicemen, Cabinet Decisions and Cultural Changes, 1917 to 1957. *316 pp. 1963. 30s.*
Workers, Unions and the State. *188 pp. 1966. (2nd Impression 1967.) 25s.*

FOREIGN AFFAIRS: THEIR SOCIAL, POLITICAL AND ECONOMIC FOUNDATIONS

Baer, Gabriel. Population and Society in the Arab East. *Translated by Hanna Szöke. 288 pp. 10 maps. 1964. 40s.*

Bonné, Alfred. State and Economics in the Middle East: A Society in Transition. *482 pp. 2nd (revised) edition 1955. (2nd Impression 1960.) 40s.*
Studies in Economic Development: with special reference to Conditions in the Under-developed Areas of Western Asia and India. *322 pp. 84 tables. 2nd edition 1960. 32s.*

Mayer, J. P. Political Thought in France from the Revolution to the Fifth Republic. *164 pp. 3rd edition (revised) 1961. 16s.*

CRIMINOLOGY

Ancel, Marc. Social Defence: A Modern Approach to Criminal Problems. *Foreword by Leon Radzinowicz. 240 pp. 1965. 32s.*

Cloward, Richard A., and Ohlin, Lloyd E. Delinquency and Opportunity: A Theory of Delinquent Gangs. *248 pp. 1961. 25s.*

Downes, David M. The Delinquent Solution. A Study in Subcultural Theory. *296 pp. 1966. 42s.*

Dunlop, A. B., and **McCabe, S.** Young Men in Detention Centres. *192 pp. 1965. 28s.*

Friedländer, Kate. The Psycho-Analytical Approach to Juvenile Delinquency: Theory, Case Studies, Treatment. *320 pp. 1947. (6th Impression 1967). 40s.*

Glueck, Sheldon and **Eleanor.** Family Environment and Delinquency. *With the statistical assistance of Rose W. Kneznek. 340 pp. 1962. (2nd Impression 1966.) 40s.*

Mannheim, Hermann. Comparative Criminology: a Text Book. *Two volumes. 442 pp. and 380 pp. 1965. (2nd Impression with corrections 1966.) 42s. a volume.*

Morris, Terence. The Criminal Area: A Study in Social Ecology. *Foreword by Hermann Mannheim. 232 pp. 25 tables. 4 maps. 1957. (2nd Impression 1966.) 28s.*

Morris, Terence and **Pauline,** assisted by **Barbara Barer.** Pentonville: A Sociological Study of an English Prison. *416 pp. 16 plates. 1963. 50s.*

Spencer, John C. Crime and the Services. *Foreword by Hermann Mannheim. 336 pp. 1954. 28s.*

Trasler, Gordon. The Explanation of Criminality. *144 pp. 1962. (2nd Impression 1967.) 20s.*

SOCIAL PSYCHOLOGY

Barbu, Zevedei. Problems of Historical Psychology. *248 pp. 1960. 25s.*

Blackburn, Julian. Psychology and the Social Pattern. *184 pp. 1945. (7th Impression 1964.) 16s.*

Fleming, C. M. Adolescence: Its Social Psychology: With an Introduction to recent findings from the fields of Anthropology, Physiology, Medicine, Psychometrics and Sociometry. *288 pp. 2nd edition (revised) 1963. (3rd Impression 1967.) 25s. Paper 12s. 6d.*

The Social Psychology of Education: An Introduction and Guide to Its Study. *136 pp. 2nd edition (revised) 1959. (4th Impression 1967.) 14s. Paper 7s. 6d.*

Homans, George C. The Human Group. *Foreword by Bernard DeVoto. Introduction by Robert K. Merton. 526 pp. 1951. (7th Impression 1968.) 35s.*

Social Behaviour: its Elementary Forms. *416 pp. 1961. (3rd Impression 1968.) 35s.*

Klein, Josephine. The Study of Groups. *226 pp. 31 figures. 5 tables. 1956. (5th Impression 1967.) 21s. Paper 9s. 6d.*

Linton, Ralph. The Cultural Background of Personality. *132 pp. 1947. (7th Impression 1968.) 18s.*

Mayo, Elton. The Social Problems of an Industrial Civilization. With an appendix on the Political Problem. *180 pp. 1949. (5th Impression 1966.) 25s.*

Ottaway, A. K. C. Learning Through Group Experience. *176 pp. 1966. (2nd Impression 1968.) 25s.*

Ridder, J. C. de. The Personality of the Urban African in South Africa. A Thematic Apperception Test Study. *196 pp. 12 plates. 1961. 25s.*

Rose, Arnold M. (Ed.). Human Behaviour and Social Processes: an Interactionist Approach. *Contributions by Arnold M. Rose, Ralph H. Turner, Anselm Strauss, Everett C. Hughes, E. Franklin Frazier, Howard S. Becker, et al. 696 pp. 1962. (2nd Impression 1968.) 70s.*

Smelser, Neil J. Theory of Collective Behaviour. *448 pp. 1962. (2nd Impression 1967.) 45s.*

Stephenson, Geoffrey M. The Development of Conscience. *128 pp. 1966. 25s.*

Young, Kimball. Handbook of Social Psychology. *658 pp. 16 figures. 10 tables. 2nd edition (revised) 1957. (3rd Impression 1963.) 40s.*

SOCIOLOGY OF THE FAMILY

Banks, J. A. Prosperity and Parenthood: A study of Family Planning among The Victorian Middle Classes. *262 pp. 1954. (3rd Impression 1968.) 28s.*

Bell, Colin R. Middle Class Families: Social and Geographical Mobility. *224 pp. 1969. 35s.*

Burton, Lindy. Vulnerable Children. *272 pp. 1968. 35s.*

Gavron, Hannah. The Captive Wife: Conflicts of Housebound Mothers. *190 pp. 1966. (2nd Impression 1966.) 25s.*

Klein, Josephine. Samples from English Cultures. *1965. (2nd Impression 1967.)*
1. Three Preliminary Studies and Aspects of Adult Life in England. *447 pp. 50s.*
2. Child-Rearing Practices and Index. *247 pp. 35s.*

Klein, Viola. Britain's Married Women Workers. *180 pp. 1965. (2nd Impression 1968.) 28s.*

McWhinnie, Alexina M. Adopted Children. How They Grow Up. *304 pp. 1967. (2nd Impression 1968.) 42s.*

Myrdal, Alva and **Klein, Viola.** Women's Two Roles: Home and Work. *238 pp. 27 tables. 1956. Revised Edition 1967. 30s. Paper 15s.*

Parsons, Talcott and **Bales, Robert F.** Family: Socialization and Interaction Process. *In collaboration with James Olds, Morris Zelditch and Philip E. Slater. 456 pp. 50 figures and tables. 1956. (3rd Impression 1968.) 45s.*

Schücking, L. L. The Puritan Family. *Translated from the German by Brian Battershaw. 212 pp. 1969. About 42s.*

7

THE SOCIAL SERVICES

Forder, R. A. (Ed.). Penelope Hall's Social Services of Modern England. *288 pp. 1969. 35s.*

George, Victor. Social Security: Beveridge and After. *258 pp. 1968. 35s.*

Goetschius, George W. Working with Community Groups. *256 pp. 1969. 35s.*

Goetschius, George W. and **Tash, Joan.** Working with Unattached Youth. *416 pp. 1967. (2nd Impression 1968.) 40s.*

Hall, M. P., and **Howes, I. V.** The Church in Social Work. A Study of Moral Welfare Work undertaken by the Church of England. *320 pp. 1965. 35s.*

Heywood, Jean S. Children in Care: the Development of the Service for the Deprived Child. *264 pp. 2nd edition (revised) 1965. (2nd Impression 1966.) 32s.*

An Introduction to Teaching Casework Skills. *190 pp. 1964. 28s.*

Jones, Kathleen. Lunacy, Law and Conscience, 1744-1845: the Social History of the Care of the Insane. *268 pp. 1955. 25s.*

Mental Health and Social Policy, 1845-1959. *264 pp. 1960. (2nd Impression 1967.) 32s.*

Jones, Kathleen and **Sidebotham, Roy.** Mental Hospitals at Work. *220 pp. 1962. 30s.*

Kastell, Jean. Casework in Child Care. *Foreword by M. Brooke Willis. 320 pp. 1962. 35s.*

Morris, Pauline. Put Away: A Sociological Study of Institutions for the Mentally Retarded. *Approx. 288 pp. 1969. About 50s.*

Nokes, P. L. The Professional Task in Welfare Practice. *152 pp. 1967. 28s.*

Rooff, Madeline. Voluntary Societies and Social Policy. *350 pp. 15 tables. 1957. 35s.*

Timms, Noel. Psychiatric Social Work in Great Britain (1939-1962). *280 pp. 1964. 32s.*

Social Casework: Principles and Practice. *256 pp. 1964. (2nd Impression 1966.) 25s. Paper 15s.*

Trasler, Gordon. In Place of Parents: A Study in Foster Care. *272 pp. 1960. (2nd Impression 1966.) 30s.*

Young, A. F., and **Ashton, E. T.** British Social Work in the Nineteenth Century. *288 pp. 1956. (2nd Impression 1963.) 28s.*

Young, A. F. Social Services in British Industry. *272 pp. 1968. 40s.*

SOCIOLOGY OF EDUCATION

Banks, Olive. Parity and Prestige in English Secondary Education: a Study in Educational Sociology. *272 pp. 1955. (2nd Impression 1963.) 32s.*

Bentwich, Joseph. Education in Israel. *224 pp. 8 pp. plates. 1965. 24s.*

Blyth, W. A. L. English Primary Education. A Sociological Description. *1965. Revised edition 1967.*
1. Schools. *232 pp. 30s. Paper 12s. 6d.*
2. Background. *168 pp. 25s. Paper 10s. 6d.*

Collier, K. G. The Social Purposes of Education: Personal and Social Values in Education. *268 pp. 1959. (3rd Impression 1965.) 21s.*

Dale, R. R., and Griffith, S. Down Stream: Failure in the Grammar School. *108 pp. 1965. 20s.*

Dore, R. P. Education in Tokugawa Japan. *356 pp. 9 pp. plates. 1965. 35s.*

Edmonds, E. L. The School Inspector. *Foreword by Sir William Alexander. 214 pp. 1962. 28s.*

Evans, K. M. Sociometry and Education. *158 pp. 1962. (2nd Impression 1966.) 18s.*

Foster, P. J. Education and Social Change in Ghana. *336 pp. 3 maps. 1965. (2nd Impression 1967.) 36s.*

Fraser, W. R. Education and Society in Modern France. *150 pp. 1963. (2nd Impression 1968.) 25s.*

Hans, Nicholas. New Trends in Education in the Eighteenth Century. *278 pp. 19 tables. 1951. (2nd Impression 1966.) 30s.*
  Comparative Education: A Study of Educational Factors and Traditions. *360 pp. 3rd (revised) edition 1958. (4th Impression 1967.) 25s. Paper 12s. 6d.*

Hargreaves, David. Social Relations in a Secondary School. *240 pp. 1967. (2nd Impression 1968.) 32s.*

Holmes, Brian. Problems in Education. A Comparative Approach. *336 pp. 1965. (2nd Impression 1967.) 32s.*

Mannheim, Karl and Stewart, W. A. C. An Introduction to the Sociology of Education. *206 pp. 1962. (2nd Impression 1965.) 21s.*

Morris, Raymond N. The Sixth Form and College Entrance. *231 pp. 1969. 40s.*

Musgrove, F. Youth and the Social Order. *176 pp. 1964. (2nd Impression 1968.) 25s. Paper 12s.*

Ortega y Gasset, José. Mission of the University. *Translated with an Introduction by Howard Lee Nostrand. 86 pp. 1946. (3rd Impression 1963.) 15s.*

Ottaway, A. K. C. Education and Society: An Introduction to the Sociology of Education. *With an Introduction by W. O. Lester Smith. 212 pp. Second edition (revised). 1962. (5th Impression 1968.) 18s. Paper 10s. 6d.*

Peers, Robert. Adult Education: A Comparative Study. *398 pp. 2nd edition 1959. (2nd Impression 1966.) 42s.*

Pritchard, D. G. Education and the Handicapped: 1760 to 1960. *258 pp. 1963. (2nd Impression 1966.) 35s.*

Richardson, Helen. Adolescent Girls in Approved Schools. *Approx. 360 pp. 1969. About 42s.*

Simon, Brian and Joan (Eds.). Educational Psychology in the U.S.S.R. *Introduction by Brian and Joan Simon. Translation by Joan Simon. Papers by D. N. Bogoiavlenski and N. A. Menchinskaia, D. B. Elkonin, E. A. Fleshner, Z. I. Kalmykova, G. S. Kostiuk, V. A. Krutetski, A. N. Leontiev, A. R. Luria, E. A. Milerian, R. G. Natadze, B. M. Teplov, L. S. Vygotski, L. V. Zankov. 296 pp. 1963. 40s.*

9

SOCIOLOGY OF CULTURE

Eppel, E. M., and M. Adolescents and Morality: A Study of some Moral Values and Dilemmas of Working Adolescents in the Context of a changing Climate of Opinion. *Foreword by W. J. H. Sprott. 268 pp. 39 tables. 1966. 30s.*

Fromm, Erich. The Fear of Freedom. *286 pp. 1942. (8th Impression 1960.) 25s. Paper 10s.* The Sane Society. *400 pp. 1956. (4th Impression 1968.) 28s. Paper 14s.*

Mannheim, Karl. Diagnosis of Our Time: Wartime Essays of a Sociologist. *208 pp. 1943. (8th Impression 1966.) 21s.* Essays on the Sociology of Culture. *Edited by Ernst Mannheim in co-operation with Paul Kecskemeti. Editorial Note by Adolph Lowe. 280 pp. 1956. (3rd Impression 1967.) 28s.*

Weber, Alfred. Farewell to European History: or The Conquest of Nihilism. *Translated from the German by R. F. C. Hull. 224 pp. 1947. 18s.*

SOCIOLOGY OF RELIGION

Argyle, Michael. Religious Behaviour. *224 pp. 8 figures. 41 tables. 1958. (4th Impression 1968.) 25s.*

Nelson, G. K. Spiritualism and Society. *313 pp. 1969. 42s.*

Stark, Werner. The Sociology of Religion. A Study of Christendom. Volume I. Established Religion. *248 pp. 1966. 35s.* Volume II. Sectarian Religion. *368 pp. 1967. 40s.* Volume III. The Universal Church. *464 pp. 1967. 45s.*

Watt, W. Montgomery. Islam and the Integration of Society. *320 pp. 1961. (3rd Impression 1966.) 35s.*

SOCIOLOGY OF ART AND LITERATURE

Beljame, Alexandre. Men of Letters and the English Public in the Eighteenth Century: 1660-1744, Dryden, Addison, Pope. *Edited with an Introduction and Notes by Bonamy Dobrée. Translated by E. O. Lorimer. 532 pp. 1948. 32s.*

Misch, Georg. A History of Autobiography in Antiquity. *Translated by E. W. Dickes. 2 Volumes. Vol. 1, 364 pp., Vol. 2, 372 pp. 1950. 45s. the set.*

Schücking, L. L. The Sociology of Literary Taste. *112 pp. 2nd (revised) edition 1966. 18s.*

Silbermann, Alphons. The Sociology of Music. *Translated from the German by Corbet Stewart. 222 pp. 1963. 32s.*

SOCIOLOGY OF KNOWLEDGE

Mannheim, Karl. Essays on the Sociology of Knowledge. *Edited by Paul Kecskemeti. Editorial note by Adolph Lowe. 352 pp. 1952. (4th Impression 1967.) 35s.*

Stark, W. America: Ideal and Reality. The United States of 1776 in Contemporary Philosophy. *136 pp. 1947. 12s.*

The Sociology of Knowledge: An Essay in Aid of a Deeper Understanding of the History of Ideas. *384 pp. 1958. (3rd Impression 1967.) 36s.*

Montesquieu: Pioneer of the Sociology of Knowledge. *244 pp. 1960. 25s.*

URBAN SOCIOLOGY

Anderson, Nels. The Urban Community: A World Perspective. *532 pp. 1960. 35s.*

Ashworth, William. The Genesis of Modern British Town Planning: A Study in Economic and Social History of the Nineteenth and Twentieth Centuries. *288 pp. 1954. (3rd Impression 1968.) 32s.*

Bracey, Howard. Neighbours: On New Estates and Subdivisions in England and U.S.A. *220 pp. 1964. 28s.*

Cullingworth, J. B. Housing Needs and Planning Policy: A Restatement of the Problems of Housing Need and "Overspill" in England and Wales. *232 pp. 44 tables. 8 maps. 1960. (2nd Impression 1966.) 28s.*

Dickinson, Robert E. City and Region: A Geographical Interpretation. *608 pp. 125 figures. 1964. (5th Impression 1967.) 60s.*

The West European City: A Geographical Interpretation. *600 pp. 129 maps. 29 plates. 2nd edition 1962. (3rd Impression 1968.) 55s.*

The City Region in Western Europe. *320 pp. Maps. 1967. 30s. Paper 14s.*

Jackson, Brian. Working Class Community: Some General Notions raised by a Series of Studies in Northern England. *192 pp. 1968. (2nd Impression 1968.) 25s.*

Jennings, Hilda. Societies in the Making: a Study of Development and Redevelopment within a County Borough. *Foreword by D. A. Clark. 286 pp. 1962. (2nd Impression 1967.) 32s.*

Kerr, Madeline. The People of Ship Street. *240 pp. 1958. 28s.*

Mann, P. H. An Approach to Urban Sociology. *240 pp. 1965. (2nd Impression 1968.) 30s.*

Morris, R. N., and **Mogey, J.** The Sociology of Housing. Studies at Berinsfield. *232 pp. 4 pp. plates. 1965. 42s.*

Rosser, C., and **Harris, C.** The Family and Social Change. A Study of Family and Kinship in a South Wales Town. *352 pp. 8 maps. 1965. (2nd Impression 1968.) 45s.*

RURAL SOCIOLOGY

Chambers, R. J. H. Settlement Schemes in Africa: A Selective Study. *Approx. 268 pp. 1969. About 50s.*

Haswell, M. R. The Economics of Development in Village India. *120 pp. 1967. 21s.*

Littlejohn, James. Westrigg: the Sociology of a Cheviot Parish. *172 pp. 5 figures. 1963. 25s.*

Williams, W. M. The Country Craftsman: A Study of Some Rural Crafts and the Rural Industries Organization in England. *248 pp. 9 figures. 1958. 25s. (Dartington Hall Studies in Rural Sociology.)*
The Sociology of an English Village: Gosforth. *272 pp. 12 figures. 13 tables. 1956. (3rd Impression 1964.) 25s.*

SOCIOLOGY OF MIGRATION

Humphreys, Alexander J. New Dubliners: Urbanization and the Irish Family. *Foreword by George C. Homans. 304 pp. 1966. 40s.*

SOCIOLOGY OF INDUSTRY AND DISTRIBUTION

Anderson, Nels. Work and Leisure. *280 pp. 1961. 28s.*

Blau, Peter M., and **Scott, W. Richard.** Formal Organizations: a Comparative approach. *Introduction and Additional Bibliography by J. H. Smith. 326 pp. 1963. (4th Impression 1969.) 35s. Paper 15s.*

Eldridge, J. E. T. Industrial Disputes. Essays in the Sociology of Industrial Relations. *288 pp. 1968. 40s.*

Hollowell, Peter G. The Lorry Driver. *272 pp. 1968. 42s.*

Jefferys, Margot, with the assistance of Winifred Moss. Mobility in the Labour Market: Employment Changes in Battersea and Dagenham. *Preface by Barbara Wootton. 186 pp. 51 tables. 1954. 15s.*

Levy, A. B. Private Corporations and Their Control. *Two Volumes. Vol. 1, 464 pp., Vol. 2, 432 pp. 1950. 80s. the set.*

Liepmann, Kate. Apprenticeship: An Enquiry into its Adequacy under Modern Conditions. *Foreword by H. D. Dickinson. 232 pp. 6 tables. 1960. (2nd Impression 1960.) 23s.*

Millerson, Geoffrey. The Qualifying Associations: a Study in Professionalization. *320 pp. 1964. 42s.*

Smelser, Neil J. Social Change in the Industrial Revolution: An Application of Theory to the Lancashire Cotton Industry, 1770-1840. *468 pp. 12 figures. 14 tables. 1959. (2nd Impression 1960.) 50s.*

Williams, Gertrude. Recruitment to Skilled Trades. *240 pp. 1957. 23s.*

Young, A. F. Industrial Injuries Insurance: an Examination of British Policy. *192 pp. 1964. 30s.*

ANTHROPOLOGY

Ammar, Hamed. Growing up in an Egyptian Village: Silwa, Province of Aswan. *336 pp. 1954. (2nd Impression 1966.) 35s.*

Crook, David and **Isabel.** Revolution in a Chinese Village: Ten Mile Inn. *230 pp. 8 plates. 1 map. 1959. (2nd Impression 1968.) 21s.*
The First Years of Yangyi Commune. *302 pp. 12 plates. 1966. 42s.*

Dickie-Clark, H. F. The Marginal Situation. A Sociological Study of a Coloured Group. *236 pp. 1966. 40s.*

Dube, S. C. Indian Village. *Foreword by Morris Edward Opler. 276 pp. 4 plates. 1955. (5th Impression 1965.) 25s.*
India's Changing Villages: Human Factors in Community Development. *260 pp. 8 plates. 1 map. 1958. (3rd Impression 1963.) 25s.*

Firth, Raymond. Malay Fishermen. Their Peasant Economy. *420 pp. 17 pp. plates. 2nd edition revised and enlarged 1966. (2nd Impression 1968.) 55s.*

Gulliver, P. H. The Family Herds. A Study of two Pastoral Tribes in East Africa, The Jie and Turkana. *304 pp. 4 plates. 19 figures. 1955. (2nd Impression with new preface and bibliography 1966.) 35s.*
Social Control in an African Society: a Study of the Arusha, Agricultural Masai of Northern Tanganyika. *320 pp. 8 plates. 10 figures. 1963. (2nd Impression 1968.) 42s.*

Ishwaran, K. Shivapur. A South Indian Village. *216 pp. 1968. 35s.*
Tradition and Economy in Village India: An Interactionist Approach. *Foreword by Conrad Arensburg. 176 pp. 1966. (2nd Impression 1968.) 25s.*

Jarvie, Ian C. The Revolution in Anthropology. *268 pp. 1964. (2nd Impression 1967.) 40s.*

Jarvie, Ian C. and **Agassi, Joseph.** Hong Kong. A Society in Transition. *396 pp. Illustrated with plates and maps. 1968. 56s.*

Little, Kenneth L. Mende of Sierra Leone. *308 pp. and folder. 1951. Revised edition 1967. 63s.*

Lowie, Professor Robert H. Social Organization. *494 pp. 1950. (4th Impression 1966.) 50s.*

Mayer, Adrian C. Caste and Kinship in Central India: A Village and its Region. *328 pp. 16 plates. 15 figures. 16 tables. 1960. (2nd Impression 1965.) 35s.*
Peasants in the Pacific: A Study of Fiji Indian Rural Society. *232 pp. 16 plates. 10 figures. 14 tables. 1961. 35s.*

Smith, Raymond T. The Negro Family in British Guiana: Family Structure and Social Status in the Villages. *With a Foreword by Meyer Fortes. 314 pp. 8 plates. 1 figure. 4 maps. 1956. (2nd Impression 1965.) 35s.*

DOCUMENTARY

Meek, Dorothea L. (Ed.). Soviet Youth: Some Achievements and Problems. *Excerpts from the Soviet Press, translated by the editor. 280 pp. 1957. 28s.*

Schlesinger, Rudolf (Ed.). Changing Attitudes in Soviet Russia.
2. The Nationalities Problem and Soviet Administration. Selected Readings on the Development of Soviet Nationalities Policies. *Introduced by the editor. Translated by W. W. Gottlieb. 324 pp. 1956. 30s.*

Reports of the Institute of Community Studies

(*Demy 8vo.*)

Cartwright, Ann. Human Relations and Hospital Care. *272 pp. 1964. 30s.*

Patients and their Doctors. A Study of General Practice. *304 pp. 1967. 40s.*

Jackson, Brian. Streaming: an Education System in Miniature. *168 pp. 1964. (2nd Impression 1966.) 21s. Paper 10s.*

Jackson, Brian and **Marsden, Dennis.** Education and the Working Class: Some General Themes raised by a Study of 88 Working-class Children in a Northern Industrial City. *268 pp. 2 folders. 1962. (4th Impression 1968.) 32s.*

Marris, Peter. Widows and their Families. *Foreword by Dr. John Bowlby. 184 pp. 18 tables. Statistical Summary. 1958. 18s.*
Family and Social Change in an African City. A Study of Rehousing in Lagos. *196 pp. 1 map. 4 plates. 53 tables. 1961. (2nd Impression 1966.) 30s.*
The Experience of Higher Education. *232 pp. 27 tables. 1964. 25s.*

Marris, Peter and **Rein, Martin.** Dilemmas of Social Reform. Poverty and Community Action in the United States. *256 pp. 1967. 35s.*

Mills, Enid. Living with Mental Illness: a Study in East London. *Foreword by Morris Carstairs. 196 pp. 1962. 28s.*

Runciman, W. G. Relative Deprivation and Social Justice. A Study of Attitudes to Social Inequality in Twentieth Century England. *352 pp. 1966. (2nd Impression 1967.) 40s.*

Townsend, Peter. The Family Life of Old People: An Inquiry in East London. *Foreword by J. H. Sheldon. 300 pp. 3 figures. 63 tables. 1957. (3rd Impression 1967.) 30s.*

Willmott, Peter. Adolescent Boys in East London. *230 pp. 1966. 30s.*
The Evolution of a Community: a study of Dagenham after forty years. *168 pp. 2 maps. 1963. 21s.*

Willmott, Peter and **Young, Michael.** Family and Class in a London Suburb. *202 pp. 47 tables. 1960. (4th Impression 1968.) 25s.*

Young, Michael. Innovation and Research in Education. *192 pp. 1965. 25s. Paper 12s. 6d.*

Young, Michael and **McGeeney, Patrick.** Learning Begins at Home. A Study of a Junior School and its Parents. *About 128 pp. 1968. 21s. Paper 14s.*

Young, Michael and **Willmott, Peter.** Family and Kinship in East London. *Foreword by Richard M. Titmuss. 252 pp. 39 tables. 1957. (3rd Impression 1965.) 28s.*

14

The British Journal of Sociology. *Edited by Terence P. Morris. Vol. 1, No. 1, March 1950 and Quarterly. Roy. 8vo., £3 annually, 15s. a number, post free. (Vols. 1-18, £8 each. Individual parts £2 10s.*

All prices are net and subject to alteration without notice

1268 H.B.